Beyond the Metrics

Beyond the Metrics

The Psychological Impact of Fitness Technology on Self-Image and Social Anxiety

Editor: Asegul Hulus

Authors: Asegul Hulus, Esat Hulus, Erman Doğan

ANTHEM PRESS

Anthem Press
An imprint of Wimbledon Publishing Company
www.anthempress.com

This edition first published in UK and USA 2026
by ANTHEM PRESS
75–76 Blackfriars Road, London SE1 8HA, UK
or PO Box 9779, London SW19 7ZG, UK
and
244 Madison Ave #116, New York, NY 10016, USA

British Library Cataloguing-in-Publication Data
A catalogue record for this book is available from the British Library.

Library of Congress Cataloging-in-Publication Data: 2025944573
A catalog record for this book has been requested.

ISBN-13: 978-1-83999-791-4 (Pbk)
ISBN-10: 1-83999-791-5 (Pbk)

Cover Credit: Designer Asegul Hulus

This title is also available as an eBook.

CONTENTS

PREFACE

This book delves into the psychological aspects of fitness technology, analyzing its impact on both physical self-perception and social body image concerns. Fitness technology has advanced significantly with the emergence of wearable devices, apps, and digital communities, playing a crucial role in promoting personal health by providing users with resources to track progress, stay motivated, and reach fitness objectives. Although these technologies promote user engagement through measurable progress and goal-setting features, they also introduce intricate psychological issues such as heightened social comparison and self-assessment pressure.

This book examines these dual effects, under the guidance of fundamental theories like Social Comparison Theory, Self-Determination Theory, and the Hierarchical Model of Physical Self-Concept. Through these frameworks, it examines the impact of fitness technology on physical self-concept, intrinsic motivation, and social physique anxiety, especially in settings that prioritize social metrics and appearance-based competition.

The concluding section, Chapters 10, 11, and 12, consolidates and expands upon these understandings through three sections. Chapter 10: Final Remarks Part 1 consolidates essential discoveries, presenting a sophisticated perspective on the advantages and drawbacks encountered by users of fitness technology. Chapter 11 Part 2 explores the wider implications of these discoveries for users, fitness professionals, developers, and policymakers, highlighting the importance of design approaches that prioritize users' mental and emotional welfare alongside physical objectives. Chapter 12 Part 3 offers recommendations and forward-looking strategies, promoting a balanced and mindful approach to fitness technology that fosters healthy engagement and safeguards users from potential psychological risks.

The main goal of this book is to encourage well-informed viewpoints on fitness technology by emphasizing the significance of ethical design, user-centered strategies, and mental health assistance within the changing digital fitness environment. It is essential to engage thoughtfully with the psychological effects of fitness technology to promote balanced and sustainable health transformations.

Chapter 1

THE DOUBLE-EDGED SWORD
OF FITNESS TECHNOLOGY

This chapter explores the inherent complexity of fitness technology, presenting it as a potent tool for self-enhancement and a potential cause of psychological stress. Through an examination of the motivational aspects of fitness technology, as well as its ability to induce social anxiety through comparison tools, this chapter presents readers with the essential duality that will be investigated in-depth throughout the book.

The fitness sector has experienced significant changes recently, as technology has altered people's attitudes toward physical well-being (Woessner et al., 2021). Users can now access detailed information about their physical activity through fitness apps, wearables, and online platforms. This data enables them to track metrics such as calorie expenditure, distance traveled, steps taken, and progress in their workouts. The progress in technology has enhanced accessibility and measurability in the realm of fitness, empowering users to acquire insights into their well-being and establish informed objectives. This capacity for self-monitoring and measuring physical performance has become a crucial aspect of the fitness journey for numerous individuals, encouraging steadfastness and responsibility (Oginni et al., 2024).

Nevertheless, the psychological effects of fitness technology are intricate and diverse. Conversely, the feedback based on data provided by these tools has the potential to improve users' physical self-perception, fostering feelings of competence, autonomy, and motivation as they monitor their development longitudinally (Codina et al., 2024). Physical self-concept, which refers to how an individual views their physical abilities, body image, and general fitness, is enhanced by the self-monitoring features of fitness technology (Marsh, 1996). Individuals who successfully reach their objectives frequently cultivate a more positive perception of themselves, leading to enhanced self-assurance and contentment with their physical capabilities (Zartaloudi et al., 2023). This drive is reinforced by functionalities that enable users to establish customized goals, empowering them to take charge of their fitness expedition. Following Self-Determination Theory, autonomy in establishing and attaining goals is vital for maintaining intrinsic motivation by promoting feelings of personal control and competence (Deci & Ryan, 1985; Ryan & Deci, 2020).

Conversely, fitness technology may also result in increased social physique anxiety, a type of anxiety arising from the perception that one's body is being evaluated by others, especially in social or performance settings (Zartaloudi et al., 2023). Many fitness applications and devices integrate social sharing capabilities, leaderboards, and online communities, enabling users to compare their accomplishments with others. For certain individuals, observing the accomplishments of others can act as a catalyst for motivation, spurring them to strive harder for their objectives. Yet, for some individuals, these comparisons might trigger feelings of inadequacy, as they see themselves as not measuring up to their peers or idealized fitness icons (Limone & Toto, 2022). Social Comparison Theory offers a valuable framework for comprehending this facet of fitness technology. Festinger (1954) introduced this theory, which posits that individuals assess their self-worth through comparisons with others, especially in the absence of clear benchmarks. Within fitness settings, this process of comparison has the potential to result in dissatisfaction with one's body and anxiety related to physical appearance, as individuals may experience pressure to conform to specific fitness norms or standards.

The influence of fitness technology on the mental well-being of users leads to a paradox. Despite the potential for self-empowerment and motivation, these tools come with risks related to social pressure and anxiety (Limone & Toto, 2022). The concept of dual influence can be exemplified by considering a hypothetical scenario involving a fitness app user aiming to raise their daily step count. When users monitor their progress and achieve milestones, they might feel a sense of achievement and self-value. However, upon sharing their accomplishment on social platforms or observing others' greater step counts, their initial contentment may decline, giving way to sentiments of inadequacy. The confidence gained through personal accomplishments may be challenged by comparing oneself to others, leading to a struggle between self-drive and self-questioning.

This paradox of self-empowerment versus self-consciousness is central to understanding the psychological impact of fitness technology. Users who engage with fitness technology must navigate between these contrasting effects, balancing the personal benefits of self-tracking and goal setting with the potential negative effects of social comparison (Codina et al., 2024). The subsequent sections delve deeper into this dual effect, examining how particular aspects of fitness technology impact physical self-concept and social physique anxiety. Through the analysis of these results, the purpose of this study is to offer a detailed insight into how individuals can utilize fitness technology to enhance their mental and physical health.

Chapter 2

THEORETICAL FOUNDATIONS

Expanding on the two viewpoints introduced in Chapter 1, this chapter establishes the conversation within fundamental psychological theories. Social Comparison Theory, Self-Determination Theory, and the Hierarchical Model of Physical Self-Concept are introduced as frameworks for comprehending the motivational and anxiety-inducing components of fitness technology. The theoretical foundation provided will guide the analysis in subsequent chapters by connecting theory with empirical data on the psychological effects of fitness technology.

The integration of fitness technology into daily life is evident, as wearable devices, fitness apps, and social media platforms motivate users to establish and monitor goals, track progress, and participate in community-centered fitness endeavors (Woessner et al., 2021). It is crucial to analyze the theoretical frameworks that elucidate human motivation, self-evaluation, and social behavior in order to comprehend the intricate psychological impacts of these technologies. The chapter elucidates three fundamental theories—Social Comparison Theory, Self-Determination Theory, and the Hierarchical Model of Physical Self-Concept—each providing significant perspectives on the impact of fitness technology on users' mental well-being, self-image, and concerns related to the body.

Social Comparison Theory

Social Comparison Theory, introduced by Leon Festinger in 1954, suggests that individuals assess their self-worth and social standing by comparing themselves to others, particularly in situations lacking clear benchmarks (Festinger, 1954). In situations where performance is highly regarded but challenging to quantify objectively—like physical appearance or fitness levels—people instinctively evaluate themselves against others to gauge their development or status. Social comparison is most effective when individuals experience uncertainty regarding their own abilities or value, prompting them to compare their achievements or setbacks with those of peers or public figures.

In the domain of fitness technology, social comparison emerges as a nearly unavoidable aspect of user engagement (Zartaloudi et al., 2023). Numerous fitness applications and wearable gadgets incorporate functionalities that enable users to share their workout accomplishments on social platforms, compare their performance metrics with others, or engage in communal challenges. The social components aim to enhance interaction and cultivate a communal atmosphere; nonetheless, they may intensify concerns regarding physical image and achievement. When individuals witness others attaining higher levels of physical fitness or upholding idealized body images, they may feel inspired, yet may also encounter self-doubt or anxiety if they view themselves as lesser in comparison (Limone & Toto, 2022).

Studies in social psychology have demonstrated that making upward comparisons, where individuals compare themselves to those they consider superior, can reduce self-esteem and evoke feelings of inadequacy, especially in areas concerning physical appearance and body image (Crusius et al., 2022). In communities centered around fitness, where users often share their workout routines and physical changes, these comparisons can intensify social physique anxiety (Zartaloudi et al., 2023). Social Comparison Theory can elucidate the heightened risk of body dissatisfaction or appearance-related anxiety in users utilizing social features of fitness technology. For certain individuals, these comparisons can act as a source of motivation, while for others, they may erode self-esteem and lead to negative psychological consequences.

Self-Determination Theory

Self-Determination Theory (SDT), formulated by Edward Deci and Richard Ryan in 1985, serves as a foundational framework for comprehending human motivation. It highlights the significance of satisfying three fundamental psychological needs: autonomy, competence, and relatedness (Deci & Ryan, 1985; Ryan & Deci, 2020). Per SDT, individuals are inherently driven to participate in activities that fulfill these needs, and their welfare is strongly linked to settings that promote autonomy, competence, and relatedness.

Fitness technology frequently satisfies these psychological needs in manners that enhance intrinsic motivation (Codina et al., 2024). For example, numerous fitness applications enable users to establish customized objectives and monitor their advancement, thereby promoting autonomy through granting users authority over their fitness endeavors. Fitness technology reinforces users' sense of competence by offering feedback on metrics like step count, calories burned, and workout intensity. Furthermore, social aspects such as friend lists, virtual challenges, and community boards promote a sense of connection by urging users to interact with individuals who have comparable fitness objectives.

Although fitness technology can enhance well-being through autonomy, competence, and relatedness, it may also impose external pressures that reduce intrinsic motivation and impact mental health negatively (Codina et al., 2024). For instance, individuals may feel anxious or doubtful if their progress does not meet perceived social standards, such as meeting performance goals or sharing achievements publicly. In such scenarios, the inherent pleasure derived from physical activity might be eclipsed by external performance expectations, potentially resulting in diminished motivation and heightened social physique anxiety (Zartaloudi et al., 2023). SDT offers a valuable framework for comprehending the motivational advantages of fitness technology while also underscoring the dangers linked with environments that prioritize competition and external validation.

Hierarchical Model of Physical Self-Concept

The Hierarchical Model of Physical Self-Concept, presented by Herbert Marsh in 1996, defines physical self-concept as a multifaceted construct consisting of distinct subdomains such as appearance, strength, endurance, and coordination (Marsh, 1996). The model proposes that individuals' self-perceptions are structured hierarchically, with a primary global physical self-concept and subordinate subdomains reinforcing this overarching perception. Every subdomain, whether related to physical appearance, athletic ability, or health, is shaped by feedback and experiences within distinct environments.

Fitness technology offers users a constant flow of data on these subdomains, allowing them to track particular aspects of their physical self-concept (Oginni et al., 2024). For example, wearable devices monitor endurance by tracking metrics such as running distance, strength by recording weightlifting achievements, and appearance by measuring body fat percentage. Receiving positive feedback on these metrics may improve self-concept by strengthening users' feelings of competence in particular areas. For instance, a person who regularly increases their running distance may enhance their overall physical self-concept through improved endurance (Codina et al., 2024).

Nevertheless, the model also underscores the possibility of adverse effects on self-perception, especially in cases where individuals do not achieve their objectives or engage in comparisons with others (Zartaloudi et al., 2023). The expectation for ongoing enhancement or surpassing peers within fitness groups may cause individuals to feel discontent with their accomplishments, despite making personal advancements. As a consequence, fitness technology has a twofold effect on physical self-perception: it can enhance users' self-assurance through positive evaluations of particular skills, yet it may also induce self-questioning if users perceive a lack of conformity with wider societal or communal norms (Limone & Toto, 2022).

Integrating Theories to Understand Fitness Technology's Impact

The theoretical frameworks of Social Comparison Theory, Self-Determination Theory, and the Hierarchical Model of Physical Self-Concept collectively offer a solid basis for examining the psychological implications of fitness technology (Codina et al., 2024; Crusius et al., 2022). Collectively, they demonstrate the impact of fitness technology on motivation, self-perception, and anxiety, frequently resulting in diverse effects influenced by individual variances and social environments.

For individuals who view fitness technology as a means of motivation and self-empowerment, these tools meet fundamental psychological needs, enhance particular skills, and encourage positive self-assessments (Ryan & Deci, 2020). However, fitness technology may lead to social physique anxiety and self-doubt for individuals facing social comparisons or performance expectations (Zartaloudi et al., 2023). The amalgamation of these theories aids in elucidating why identical technological attributes can empower certain users and induce psychological stress in others.

The convergence of these theoretical frameworks elucidates how the influence of fitness technology on users is regulated by variances in motivation, self-concept, and susceptibility to social comparison (Limone & Toto, 2022). For example, individuals with robust intrinsic drive may demonstrate reduced susceptibility to social comparison elements, directing their attention toward personal growth and skill enhancement (Deci & Ryan, 1985). Alternatively, individuals with a higher sensitivity to social evaluation might experience a decline in intrinsic motivation due to the existence of comparative elements, resulting in heightened anxiety and decreased pleasure in physical activities (Festinger, 1954).

It is essential to comprehend these theoretical interactions in order to create fitness technology that enhances psychological well-being, as opposed to hindering it (Woessner et al., 2021). When examining the interaction of social comparison processes with motivation and self-concept, developers and professionals have the opportunity to design elements that enhance autonomous motivation and reduce the potential for negative social comparison. This could entail granting users increased authority over social sharing functionalities, prioritizing personal growth over social rivalry, and assisting in cultivating a robust, diverse physical self-perception (Oginni et al., 2024).

Moreover, these theories propose that the psychological influence of fitness technology is variable and reliant on the implementation of features and user interaction. For instance, social elements focusing on collaboration and assistance instead of rivalry could fulfill the need for relatedness without provoking adverse social contrasts (Codina et al., 2024). Moreover, monitoring functionalities that emphasize enhancements across various physical aspects could contribute to a stronger and more enduring physical self-perception than systems that concentrate solely on metrics related to appearance (Marsh, 1996).

As the field of fitness technology advances, these conceptual frameworks offer essential direction for comprehending and enhancing its psychological influence. By taking into account the interaction of social comparison processes, basic psychological needs, and physical self-concept, developers and professionals can design fitness technology tools that are more supportive and effective. Subsequent chapters expand on these theoretical underpinnings by exploring particular results from both quantitative and qualitative studies, providing perspectives on the impact of fitness technology on users' mental health in real-life scenarios.

Chapter 3
METHODOLOGICAL APPROACH

This chapter delineates a mixed-methods research strategy that integrates quantitative and qualitative data for a thorough analysis of the psychological aspects of fitness technology. This section outlines the research design, participant characteristics, and analytical approaches employed, offering a methodological perspective to enrich comprehension of how fitness technology impacts users' self-concept and anxiety levels. The robustness of this methodology supports the conclusions presented in the following sections.

This study utilizes a mixed-methods approach to investigate the psychological impact of fitness technology on physical self-concept and social physique anxiety, combining quantitative and qualitative data. This integrated method enables a thorough examination of the impact of fitness technology on users' self-perceptions and body-related anxieties according to Zartaloudi et al. (2023). The quantitative aspect examines the connections among the use of fitness technology, physical self-concept, and social physique anxiety, whereas the qualitative aspect delves into users' individual experiences and perspectives. This chapter details the research design, participant demographics, data collection methods, and analysis techniques.

Research Design and Research Question

The mixed-methods design was chosen to encompass both quantifiable relationships and nuanced personal experiences related to the use of fitness technology in response to the research question:

"How does fitness technology, including fitness apps, wearables, and social media, influence physical self-concept in individuals who regularly engage in fitness or bodybuilding?"

Quantitative data was gathered through the utilization of psychometric scales specifically created to evaluate physical self-concept and social physique anxiety, facilitating statistical examination of the research hypotheses. Concurrently, qualitative data was collected via semi-structured interviews, capturing users' subjective experiences, motivations, challenges, and emotional responses. This integrated strategy tackles the psychological impact of fitness technology by addressing the "what" and "how," while delving into the deeper contextual reasons, the "why." Gernigon et al. (2023) suggest that combining quantitative and qualitative data enhances the validity of studies on complex psychological phenomena and enables a more nuanced understanding of the results.

Participants

The research enlisted 40 male subjects aged 18–40 using convenience sampling from gym and fitness center locations. This particular demographic was selected due to the fact that men who regularly participate in fitness or bodybuilding serve as a key user segment for fitness technology and often encounter challenges associated with physical self-perception and social physique anxiety (Zartaloudi et al., 2023). Additionally, recent research indicates that men involved in fitness-oriented activities are increasingly affected by body image concerns, contrary to the previous focus on women's experiences with body image and social physique anxiety (Limone & Toto, 2022). By concentrating on this specific demographic, the research fills a void in the existing literature and provides valuable perspectives on the encounters of male users in fitness environments.

All the individuals involved were habitual users of fitness technology, such as fitness apps, wearable trackers, or specialized social media platforms for fitness (Woessner et al., 2021). By choosing individuals with significant expertise in utilizing these technologies, the research ensures relevance and thoroughness in investigating the psychological effects of fitness technology. Efforts were undertaken to ensure diversity in the sample based on fitness levels and frequency of technology use, as these variables could impact users' self-perceptions and reactions to social elements. A group of 20 participants from the pool was chosen for qualitative interviews to provide in-depth insights into individual interactions with fitness technology.

Quantitative Data Collection

Quantitative data was gathered through the utilization of two validated psychometric scales, namely the Marsh Physical Self-Description Inventory (PSDI) and the Social Physique Anxiety Scale (SPAS). The PSDI, created by Marsh in 1996, evaluates various aspects of physical self-concept, encompassing domains like strength, appearance, flexibility, and endurance. This scale offers a thorough insight into participants' self-assessments of their physical capabilities and body image, aligning well with the objectives of this study. The SPAS, created by Marsh (1996), assesses the level of anxiety individuals feel when they perceive scrutiny of their bodies by others, thus addressing key components of social physique anxiety crucial for comprehending the psychological impacts of fitness technology in environments focusing on appearance and performance.

In addition to these scales, a self-report survey was created to evaluate participants' interaction with fitness technology (Woll et al., 2023). The survey collected information on the frequency and level of technology utilization, various types of technology employed such as fitness applications, wearable devices, and social media, as well as how much participants shared their fitness achievements with others (Oginni et al., 2024). The integration of these strategies facilitated a thorough examination of the impact of various technology usages on physical self-perception and social physique anxiety, laying the foundation for correlation and regression analyses.

Qualitative Data Collection

Qualitative data was collected via semi-structured interviews with a subgroup of 20 participants selected from the broader sample. The semi-structured interview format facilitated flexibility, allowing participants to openly discuss their experiences while ensuring the exploration of key themes pertinent to the research question (Ratan et al., 2019). The interview questions examined participants' utilization of fitness technology, their motivations and objectives, their reactions to feedback and social sharing functionalities, and their encounters with social physique anxiety (Codina et al., 2024). For example, participants were tasked with explaining the impact of monitoring progress on their self-perception, detailing feelings of judgment or self-consciousness when discussing accomplishments, and assessing the influence of social comparison on their fitness journey. The qualitative data enhances the comprehension of the psychological effects of fitness technology, offering depth and detail to the quantitative results.

Data Analysis

Descriptive and inferential statistical methods were employed to analyze the quantitative data collected from the PSDI, SPAS, and self-report technology use questionnaire in order to test the study's hypotheses.

The study presents four fundamental hypotheses derived from the previously outlined theoretical framework. The initial hypothesis proposes a direct correlation between the utilization of fitness technology and one's physical self-perception. Based on the Hierarchical Model of Physical Self-Concept (Marsh, 1996), this hypothesis suggests that feedback from fitness technology, such as progress tracking and performance metrics, boosts users' perceptions of their physical abilities. Given that consistent interaction enhances users' sense of competence and self-esteem, improvements in physical self-concept are anticipated through advancements in strength, endurance, and coordination. This implies a favorable correlation between the utilization of fitness technology and social physique anxiety. According to Social Comparison Theory (Festinger, 1954), this hypothesis posits that the social elements of fitness technology, particularly those facilitating peer comparison via tools like leaderboards or transformation visuals, may elevate body-related anxiety. When individuals are under pressure to conform to external expectations in public fitness settings, they might encounter increased anxiety regarding their physical aesthetics (Zartaloudi et al., 2023).

The third hypothesis pertains to the correlation between physical self-concept and social physique anxiety. This hypothesis is based on the concept that individuals who have a heightened awareness of their physical capabilities are prone to experiencing increased confidence, leading to a reduction in anxiety associated with social comparison (Marsh, 1996). It is suggested that an improved physical self-concept can act as a protective barrier, decreasing vulnerability to societal pressures regarding body image.

The fourth hypothesis explores the mediating role in the association between physical self-concept and social physique anxiety. This dual impact emphasizes the role of fitness technology in enhancing self-image through feedback on personal advancement, while also intensifying anxiety through encouraging social comparison and perceived social pressure. Therefore, fitness technology is suggested to serve as a mediator, illustrating its intricate influence on users' self-concept and social physique anxiety (Zartaloudi et al., 2023).

Descriptive statistics, such as means, standard deviations, and ranges, were computed to present an overview of participants' scores on the PSDI and SPAS, providing insights into broad patterns in physical self-concept and social physique anxiety. Pearson correlation analysis was performed to investigate the connections among important variables, such as utilization of fitness technology, various dimensions of physical self-concept, and social physique anxiety. This analysis aided in the investigation of hypotheses regarding the connections between technology usage, self-concept, and anxiety. Linear regression analysis was conducted to delve deeper into the predictive abilities of specific subdomains of physical self-concept on social physique anxiety. The study revealed the most influential dimensions, like strength and appearance, in predicting social physique anxiety, leading to a deeper comprehension of the impact of fitness technology on psychological well-being (Zartaloudi et al., 2023).

The qualitative data obtained from interviews underwent thematic analysis, a methodology enabling researchers to categorize and recognize recurring themes among participants' feedback (Braun & Clarke, 2006). Braun and Clarke's (2006) guidelines for thematic analysis were selected due to their capacity to identify patterns and respect individual experiences, rendering them suitable for investigating intricate psychological phenomena. The analysis commenced with an initial review of the interview transcripts to acquaint the researcher with the data, then proceeded with the development of preliminary codes that highlighted core concepts. The codes were categorized into overarching themes, including "technology as a motivator," "social comparison and anxiety," and "enhanced self-awareness," reflecting the essence of participants' experiences (Crusius et al., 2022). The themes were subsequently examined alongside the quantitative results to pinpoint areas of agreement and disagreement, facilitating a comprehensive analysis of the research inquiries.

Ethical Considerations

The study followed ethical guidelines set by the British Psychological Society (BPS) and the British Educational Research Association (BERA) (British Educational Research Association, 2018; The British Psychological Society, 2018). Ethical considerations were crucial in the research design, data collection, and reporting processes, given the emphasis on sensitive topics like body image, social comparison, and anxiety.

All individuals involved were thoroughly briefed on the objectives, methods, and their entitlements of the research, in accordance with BPS directives on informed consent. Participants were provided with a comprehensive explanation of the study's aims and were notified that their involvement was completely voluntary, allowing them to withdraw at any point without facing any repercussions (British Educational Research Association, 2018). Before commencing the study, written informed consent was acquired to ensure participants comprehended their rights and the research's potential extent. Participants were ensuring that all gathered data would be kept anonymous and confidential, aligning with the focus on respecting participant privacy and safeguarding data protection by both BPS and BERA.

Moreover, steps were implemented to account for the potential psychological sensitivity of the study's subject matter (Limone & Toto, 2022). In accordance with BPS protocols on research with potentially vulnerable individuals, participants were provided the choice to refrain from answering any interview queries that caused discomfort or distress. The researcher also offered participants access to support resources and contact details for mental health services, ensuring that those facing psychological distress could seek professional help (The British Psychological Society, 2018). Aligned with BERA's dedication to protecting the welfare of research participants through risk reduction and provision of support information.

During the research procedure, data was securely stored on devices protected by passwords that were only accessible to the research team (British Educational Research Association, 2018). Prior to analysis, all identifiable information in the data was eliminated, and pseudonyms were utilized when presenting the results to safeguard the anonymity of the participants. Furthermore, following BPS and BERA guidelines, the presentation of findings was structured to prevent the disclosure of any personal information or sensitive data that could jeopardize the confidentiality of participants.

The research centered on the psychological effects of fitness technology (Woessner et al., 2021) and social physique anxiety (Zartaloudi et al., 2023), necessitating careful consideration of participant welfare during data gathering. Careful attention was paid to the possibility of triggering body image concerns or anxiety during interviews. The research team received training to identify signs of distress and had established protocols for directing participants to suitable support services, if necessary (The British Psychological Society, 2018).

The study design included scheduled interactions with participants to address any concerns they had about their involvement or data usage (Codina et al., 2024). The continuous conversation played a key role in maintaining participants' sense of support and respect during the research, all while upholding the scientific rigor of the study.

The ethical oversight ensured that the research followed the highest ethical standards, showcasing the commitment of both BPS and BERA to fostering respectful, responsible, and protective research settings (British Educational Research Association, 2018; The British Psychological Society, 2018). By meticulously addressing ethical concerns at every stage of the research, the study was able to provide significant insights into the psychological impacts of fitness technology while safeguarding the well-being and privacy of participants.

By combining precise quantitative measurement with thorough qualitative exploration, all while upholding stringent ethical standards, this methodological approach established a comprehensive framework for examining the impact of fitness technology on users' physical self-concept and social physique anxiety. The subsequent sections will showcase the results derived from this methodological strategy, providing perspectives on the favorable and adverse psychological effects of utilizing fitness technology.

Chapter 4

THE POSITIVE SIDE—MOTIVATION AND ENHANCED PHYSICAL SELF-CONCEPT

This chapter commences by shifting from methodology to findings, focusing on the positive psychological effects of fitness technology. It explores how characteristics such as self-monitoring and feedback aid in users' physical self-perception and intrinsic drive, in accordance with Self-Determination Theory. By highlighting the advantages of fitness technology, it paves the way for the forthcoming conversation on its divergent impacts.

The findings of this study demonstrate a notable favorable influence of fitness technology on users' physical self-concept and intrinsic motivation (Codina et al., 2024). Fitness technology functioned as a potent tool for self-enhancement for numerous participants, enabling them to establish personal objectives, monitor advancements, and observe tangible proof of their accomplishments. The organized, data-focused aspect of fitness technology promotes the establishment of goals, offering users precise, measurable indicators that encourage them to maintain regularity in their fitness regimens (Oginni et al., 2024). This section delves into the factors that contribute to this beneficial impact, connecting the results to pertinent theoretical frameworks and demonstrating the ways in which these effects are reflected in the daily lives of users.

Strengthening Physical Self-Concept through Feedback

The feedback mechanisms integrated into fitness technology are essential in strengthening users' self-perceptions of their physical capabilities (Marsh, 1996). For example, wearable devices like smartwatches and fitness trackers provide users with real-time updates on various metrics such as step count, calories burned, heart rate, and distance covered, enabling users to track their progress over time. Participants indicated that the ongoing feedback had a positive impact on their perception of competence, a crucial aspect of physical self-concept. As individuals noticed quantifiable enhancements in their physical fitness, they started to view themselves as more competent, self-assured, and adaptable (Woessner et al., 2021).

A participant, who utilized a fitness application to monitor his weightlifting advancements, expressed the motivational uplift he experienced upon achieving a personal goal: "Witnessing a continuous increase in numbers each week greatly impacts me." This instance demonstrates how technology can promote a more favorable physical self-image through enabling users to observe concrete indicators of progress (Codina et al., 2024). These metrics often act as a source of motivation, affirming their hard work and strengthening their confidence in their physical abilities.

This discovery closely corresponds with Self-Determination Theory, which suggests that competence, one of the three fundamental psychological needs, is crucial for intrinsic motivation. Deci and Ryan (1985) suggested that individuals experience motivation when they view themselves as competent and capable in their endeavors. Through offering users data that mirrors their accomplishments, fitness technology meets the need for competence, consequently boosting intrinsic motivation (Ryan & Deci, 2020). The feedback provided by fitness apps and devices serves as a continual reminder of users' progress, fostering sustained motivation through illustrating that their actions result in significant achievements.

Encouraging Goal-Setting and Persistence

The organized and goal-driven characteristics of fitness technology have been identified as a crucial element in fostering perseverance and dedication to fitness regimens (Codina et al., 2024). By enabling users to establish precise and measurable objectives—like boosting daily step counts, finishing a set number of workouts weekly, or hitting a target heart rate during cardio sessions—fitness technology provides users with a defined route to follow. The capability to monitor gradual advancements toward these objectives aids in maintaining user commitment, as it allows them to observe the diminishing gap between their present position and their goals (Oginni et al., 2024).

Another participant emphasized the motivational influence of this goal-setting attribute: "I establish a weekly running distance goal, and the app monitors it for me." The goal-setting feature of the app motivated the participant by fostering accountability (Codina et al., 2024). The awareness that the application would monitor and document his advancement motivated him to uphold his obligations, especially during times of reduced motivation.

Self-Determination Theory provides an explanation for the correlation between goal-setting and intrinsic motivation (Ryan & Deci, 2020). By granting users the freedom to establish and work toward personal objectives, fitness technology empowers them to exert authority over their fitness progression, meeting the requirement for autonomy. This independence, along with an increasing feeling of accomplishment from achieving these objectives, fosters an atmosphere conducive to intrinsic motivation. Users are motivated by internal dedication to self-improvement, rather than external influences, and this drive is consistently supported by progress-tracking data.

Building Self-Efficacy and Psychological Resilience

Furthermore, fitness technology not only enhances one's physical self-image but also fosters self-efficacy and psychological resilience (Limone & Toto, 2022). Self-efficacy, defined as the belief in one's capability to accomplish certain goals, is a vital element in motivation and psychological strength. Numerous individuals found that using technology to track their fitness progress helped them achieve personal milestones, leading to increased self-efficacy and resilience in overcoming obstacles.

A participant described how attaining a long-term goal with the assistance of his fitness tracker enhanced his ability to overcome challenges: "Initially, accomplishing even minor objectives seemed overwhelming when I began using the tracker." The experience of this participant illustrates how fitness technology can enhance users' confidence in overcoming challenges (Zartaloudi et al., 2023). As individuals establish a history of achievements, they begin to perceive obstacles as surmountable, leading to a positive influence on their self-perception and overall mental health.

According to Albert Bandura's theory of self-efficacy, individuals' confidence in their capacity to achieve success affects their resilience, diligence, and emotional reactions toward obstacles (Bandura, 1977). Fitness technology enhances users' self-efficacy by offering measurable milestones and achievements, equipping them with the psychological resources necessary to persevere in their objectives despite obstacles (Zartaloudi et al., 2023). This enhancement in self-efficacy has a broad impact on various aspects of life for numerous users, cultivating a more resilient mindset in general.

Practical Applications and Implications for Fitness Technology Design

The beneficial effects of fitness technology on motivation and physical self-perception imply various practical uses for individuals, fitness experts, and innovators (Woessner et al., 2021). Users who comprehend the impact of fitness technology on motivation may be able to utilize these tools more efficiently. The psychological benefits of fitness technology can be maximized by setting realistic goals, emphasizing personal progress, and consistently reflecting on accomplishments (Codina et al., 2024). For example, individuals who commemorate achieving milestones could enhance their self-perception and self-confidence, thereby cultivating continuous motivation in their fitness endeavor.

Fitness professionals may also benefit from the positive impact of fitness technology by motivating clients to monitor their progress and establish realistic goals (Oginni et al., 2024). By aiding clients in interpreting their data to prioritize personal development over comparison, fitness professionals can steer individuals toward healthier self-perceptions. Furthermore, it may be advisable for fitness experts to suggest particular applications or gadgets providing personalized feedback and highlighting gradual progress, thereby facilitating clients' interaction with technology in ways conducive to their mental health (Woessner et al., 2021).

The results underscore the significance for developers to create technology that emphasizes personal development, goal-setting, and positive feedback mechanisms (Limone & Toto, 2022). Characteristics that enable users to establish personalized, gradual objectives could enhance sustained motivation, whereas notifications of accomplishments or updates on progress can strengthen feelings of proficiency. Furthermore, developers may wish to include characteristics that promote self-reflection on personal accomplishments, like reminders to assess weekly or monthly advancements (Oginni et al., 2024). By focusing on personal development rather than comparing oneself to others, fitness technology can assist in promoting a healthier and more positive self-perception among its users.

Conclusion

The results outlined in this chapter illustrate the notable benefits of fitness technology on users' physical self-perception, drive, and belief in their abilities (Codina et al., 2024). Through feedback, goal-setting, and progress tracking, fitness technology fulfills essential psychological needs, allowing users to achieve personal growth and empowerment (Ryan & Deci, 2020). By empowering users to oversee their fitness progress and enhancing their feelings of capability, these tools encourage intrinsic drive and mental strength (Marsh, 1996).

Nevertheless, as the following chapter will explore, the influence of fitness technology is not consistently favorable. While these tools have the potential to improve motivation and self-esteem, they may also bring about challenges linked to social comparison and anxiety, as highlighted by Zartaloudi et al. (2023). The impact of fitness technology is multifaceted, necessitating thoughtful deliberation from users, experts, and developers. This comprehensive grasp of both advantages and possible disadvantages lays the groundwork for creating fitness technology solutions that are more efficient and psychologically supportive (Crusius et al., 2022).

Through analyzing the benefits of fitness technology, this book obtains valuable insights on how to enhance these tools to enhance users' psychological well-being and physical health objectives. Moving forward, the challenge is to preserve these advantageous elements while mitigating the possible adverse effects discussed in upcoming sections.

Chapter 5

THE NEGATIVE SIDE—SOCIAL COMPARISON AND SOCIAL PHYSIQUE ANXIETY

This chapter discusses the counterbalance to positive outcomes by examining fitness technology's impact on social physique anxiety and stress through social comparison. This chapter utilizes Social Comparison Theory to elucidate how social and competitive factors can redirect individuals' attention from personal growth to seeking external approval, thereby introducing possible psychological hazards. The dual impact plays a central role in the nuanced perspective that this book aims to offer.

Fitness technology has the potential to boost motivation and self-perception, yet its social and comparative aspects can pose notable psychological hurdles for numerous users (Codina et al., 2024). The data shows that certain features, especially those related to social sharing and peer comparison, heighten social physique anxiety, a type of anxiety triggered by the perception of others judging one's physical appearance (Zartaloudi et al., 2023). This section delves into how the social dimensions of fitness technology create settings where individuals might experience self-consciousness, anxiety, or pressure to conform to certain social fitness norms. The results are situated within Social Comparison Theory and relevant psychological studies, emphasizing how the design of the technology may at times compromise users' self-esteem and welfare.

The Rise of Social Comparison in Fitness Technology

Social comparison has emerged as a nearly inevitable element of fitness technology (Crusius et al., 2022). Many fitness applications and devices, such as Strava, MyFitnessPal, and wearable trackers like Fitbit, incorporate social functionalities enabling users to share their workout outcomes, compare their achievements with friends or community members, and engage in challenges (Woessner et al., 2021). These characteristics are intended to cultivate a feeling of unity and offer social encouragement. According to participants in the study, this feature of fitness technology has the potential to result in heightened body dissatisfaction and anxiety if users feel they are not meeting others' accomplishments.

A participant elaborated on how the integration of social media into his fitness application heightened his self-awareness regarding his physical appearance: "It is not solely about enhancing performance but also about attaining a particular aesthetic." The experience of this participant highlights the influence of upward social comparison, in which individuals compare themselves to those they view as more successful or physically attractive. Based on Festinger's (1954) Social Comparison Theory, individuals engage in comparisons to assess their self-worth, which can result in negative self-evaluations if they perceive themselves as lacking. In environments focused on fitness technology, the emphasis on physical performance and body image may result in increased social physique anxiety, as users may feel compelled to meet idealized fitness norms (Limone & Toto, 2022).

Quantitative Findings on Social Physique Anxiety

The quantitative analysis in this study indicates a notable correlation between the frequency of fitness technology utilization and levels of social physique anxiety reported, especially in users who interact with social sharing and comparison functionalities (Zartaloudi et al., 2023). According to the Social Physique Anxiety Scale (SPAS) scores, individuals who often share their fitness accomplishments or track others' advancements experienced greater body image discomfort (Marsh, 1996). This discovery indicates that increased participation in social aspects correlates with a higher likelihood of feeling anxious about others' perceptions of one's physical appearance.

As an illustration, individuals who regularly monitored their position on application leaderboards or exchanged their exercise outcomes with acquaintances disclosed experiencing sentiments of inadequacy and self-awareness, notably if their achievement measures were inferior to those of their counterparts (Limone & Toto, 2022). A participant conveyed their frustration regarding this experience: "I used to feel content with my progress until I began comparing my results with those of others." The response underscores how competitive aspects of fitness technology may unintentionally redirect users' attention from personal development to external affirmation (Crusius et al., 2022). Through placing users in a comparative context, these platforms frequently uphold societal norms that prioritize physical attractiveness, leading to social physique anxiety among users who believe they cannot meet these standards.

The Role of Body Image and Appearance-Related Pressure

Another notable theme that surfaced from the data was the perceived pressure users experience to portray an idealized image of themselves, especially in social media environments (Zartaloudi et al., 2023). Fitness applications that promote progress photos, body measurements, and weight tracking tend to prioritize appearance-based indicators, potentially intensifying worries about body image. Numerous participants expressed anxiety regarding sharing progress photos, concerned about potential judgment for not meeting specific physical standards.

A participant expressed her unease with this aspect by mentioning, "I fear that not appearing toned or fit in my progress pictures might lead others to doubt my dedication." This account is consistent with research in the field of body image psychology, indicating that environments that prioritize physical appearance may heighten social physique anxiety, particularly in situations where individuals perceive themselves being judged by others (Marsh, 1996). For these individuals, fitness technology shifts focus from personal well-being to meeting societal standards of physical beauty, leading to a cycle of comparison and self-judgment that can erode self-confidence.

This phenomenon is consistent with conclusions drawn from studies in social psychology (Festinger, 1954), showing that environments emphasizing appearance can heighten body dissatisfaction, especially for individuals sensitive to social evaluations. The continual exposure to the accomplishments of others and the expectation to adhere to visible fitness norms may result in unfavorable self-evaluations, as individuals sense an obligation to conform to identical aesthetic standards. These settings can lead to social physique anxiety by promoting an external locus of assessment, in which individuals' self-esteem relies on the validation of others and the perception of achievement, rather than on internal contentment with personal advancement (Ryan & Deci, 2020).

Qualitative Insights on Anxiety and Social Validation

The qualitative data provides additional insight into how the social aspects of fitness technology can redirect users' attention from internal drive to external confirmation (Codina et al., 2024). Some participants observed that their initial reason for joining fitness communities was to seek motivation, but over time, they found themselves becoming more competitive and anxious about their progress. A specific case involves a participant who explained how his initial eagerness to take part in a fitness challenge turned into a focus on outdoing others.

The transition from internal drive to external approval is essential in comprehending the psychological effects of fitness technology. In Self-Determination Theory, it is highlighted that intrinsic motivation remains strong when individuals pursue objectives based on personal interest and fulfillment rather than external pressures (Deci & Ryan, 1985; Ryan & Deci, 2020). Nevertheless, if users experience pressure to meet expectations for social validation, their motivation could shift toward external factors, potentially leading to increased susceptibility to feelings of inadequacy and anxiety. Fitness technology could transition for these individuals from an empowering tool to a stress-inducing factor, fueled by social components that cultivate a culture of constant comparison and performance pressure (Zartaloudi et al., 2023).

Implications for Users, Professionals, and Developers

The results of this research underscore the importance of adopting a well-rounded strategy toward utilizing fitness technology, which aims to reduce the negative impacts of social comparison while capitalizing on the motivational advantages of community encouragement (Woessner et al., 2021). Users can benefit from comprehending the psychological impacts of social comparison to engage more consciously with these platforms. Instead of depending on leaderboards or social media validation, users could concentrate on personal growth by establishing achievable goals that resonate with their values and capabilities. Implementing boundaries regarding social functions, such as restricting exposure to comparison-focused elements of applications, could assist individuals in fostering a more balanced interaction with fitness technology (Limone & Toto, 2022).

Fitness experts are essential in assisting clients in managing these societal influences (Oginni et al., 2024). Trainers can steer clients toward healthier self-perceptions by promoting personal achievements over social metrics. Fitness professionals might also support methods that prioritize internal motivation over competition, especially for clients who are vulnerable to social physique anxiety (Ryan & Deci, 2020). Offering advice on establishing personal, performance-driven goals instead of appearance-centric targets could assist individuals in finding greater fulfillment in their workout routines, diminishing the impact of external comparisons.

For developers, these results emphasize the significance of creating fitness technology that enhances users' intrinsic motivation and mitigates social comparison risks (Codina et al., 2024). Developers may wish to contemplate integrating elements that emphasize personal development and introspection rather than competitive measures, like private goal monitoring, personal achievement alerts, or thoughtful cues that prompt users to acknowledge their advancements regardless of external factors (Limone & Toto, 2022). Moreover, restricting social sharing options or enabling users to personalize the elements of their progress they want to share publicly can enhance user interaction with the technology in ways conducive to mental health. Developers can foster healthier and more balanced engagement by creating platforms that prioritize individual growth over appearance-based validation (Woessner et al., 2021).

Conclusion

The information presented in this chapter indicates that although fitness technology can encourage motivation, its social and comparative aspects may also lead to social physique anxiety and appearance-related pressures (Zartaloudi et al., 2023). Through social comparison (Festinger, 1954; Crusius et al., 2022), users may shift from intrinsic motivation to external validation, making them more susceptible to self-doubt, stress, and body dissatisfaction. The shift from internal to external motivation is consistent with the forecasts of Self-Determination Theory regarding the influence of external forces on mental health (Ryan & Deci, 2020).

The results underscore various significant issues related to the influence of social aspects in fitness technology platforms. Initially, the prevalent influence of social comparison on these platforms (Limone & Toto, 2022) seems to compel users to consistently evaluate themselves in comparison to others. This behavior is associated with a rise in social physique anxiety, as individuals interact more with these social aspects, leading to an escalation of their concerns regarding physical appearance (Zartaloudi et al., 2023). Furthermore, the expectation to adhere to ideal fitness standards and appearance-based measurements, as highlighted by Marsh (1996), prompts individuals to synchronize their fitness objectives and advancements with frequently impractical societal norms. Hence, this comparison in social settings results in a transition from internal to external drive, as individuals start to prioritize approval from others over personal goals (Marsh, 1996). Together, these aspects highlight the intricacies and psychological impacts of the social components within fitness technology.

These results underscore the importance of using fitness technology mindfully, focusing on balancing community involvement with personal development. By acknowledging the dangers linked to social comparison, individuals in various roles can work together to cultivate fitness programs that enhance both physical and mental health (Oginni et al., 2024). Future advancements in fitness technology should prioritize functionalities that enhance intrinsic motivation and offer users increased control over their social interactions, in order to sustain the advantages of community support while reducing the potential negative impact of comparison and assessment.

Moving forward, the challenge is to establish fitness technology settings that promote connection and assistance while avoiding the adverse impacts of social comparison. This necessitates a delicate equilibrium between social aspects and tools for personal growth, along with heightened user awareness regarding the potential psychological effects of various interaction patterns (Marsh, 1996). By employing considerate design and informed utilization, fitness technology can more effectively fulfill its main objective of aiding users' health and well-being, encompassing both physical and psychological aspects.

Chapter 6

BALANCING THE DUAL IMPACT—HOW TO USE FITNESS TECHNOLOGY RESPONSIBLY

Following the examination of positive and negative effects, this chapter provides actionable approaches for users, fitness professionals, and developers to interact with fitness technology in a well-rounded way. The chapter highlights the importance of responsible usage and design practices to enhance benefits and reduce psychological risks, providing a framework to promote users' mental well-being during their fitness endeavors.

Prior sections have shown that fitness technology can act as a motivator and also play a role in social physique anxiety, contingent upon usage and user traits (Codina et al., 2024). The dual influence of fitness technology highlights the significance of deliberate involvement for users striving to reach their fitness objectives and for experts and creators striving to establish settings that promote mental and physical health (Zartaloudi et al., 2023). This chapter provides practical strategies for users to maximize the benefits of fitness technology while reducing its associated risks. It further offers valuable information for fitness professionals seeking to effectively assist their clients and for developers aiming to craft user-centered, psychologically supportive designs.

Recommendations for Users: Prioritizing Personal Growth over Social Validation

For individual users, establishing a positive relationship with fitness technology involves viewing it as a tool for self-enhancement rather than a tool for social comparison (Crusius et al., 2022). The data indicates that social sharing and competition can serve as sources of motivation for certain individuals, yet they may elevate social physique anxiety for others, particularly when individuals sense a need to conform to expected norms of physical fitness and appearance (Limone & Toto, 2022). It is crucial to prioritize personal growth over seeking external validation to sustain motivation and lower anxiety levels.

One effective approach involves individuals establishing specific personal goals independent of social validation (Ryan & Deci, 2020). By concentrating on metrics that correspond with their personal fitness values—such as strength, endurance, or flexibility—rather than metrics centered on appearance, individuals can cultivate a sense of proficiency and self-esteem that is not reliant on social comparisons. For instance, individuals may find it advantageous to monitor performance-oriented accomplishments, such as completing a set distance or lifting a particular amount of weight, as opposed to establishing objectives linked to physical appearance, such as shedding weight or enhancing muscle tone (Crusius et al., 2022; Marsh, 1996). Performance goals offer a more measurable approach and can redirect attention from physical appearance to physical capability, potentially alleviating social physique anxiety.

By reducing interaction with social aspects like leaderboards or community rankings, users who are prone to social comparison can also experience advantages (Woessner et al., 2021). By electing to maintain certain elements of their fitness journey in private, individuals can uphold a sense of autonomy and concentrate on their personal advancement. For example, choosing not to share progress photos or establish personal milestones using the app's private tracking capabilities could help lessen the tendency to make comparisons with others. Engaging in self-reflection activities, like keeping a fitness journal or establishing weekly objectives, could also boost individuals' inner drive by enabling them to acknowledge and appreciate their personal accomplishments regardless of external judgments (Crusius et al., 2022).

Guidance for Fitness Professionals: Supporting Clients' Intrinsic Motivation

Fitness professionals, including trainers and coaches, play a significant role in guiding clients toward healthier and more balanced interactions with fitness technology (Oginni et al., 2024). As reputable authorities in clients' fitness endeavors, professionals can assist clients in leveraging the benefits of fitness technology while minimizing the psychological risks linked to social comparison and performance pressure. According to the data, clients are typically more driven by personal accomplishments than by competitive achievements, highlighting the need for professionals to prioritize personal progress (Codina et al., 2024).

An effective strategy for professionals is to prompt clients to establish attainable, personal goals that align with their distinct capabilities and preferences (Ryan & Deci, 2020). By working together with clients to determine objectives that are in line with their personal motivations, such as enhancing cardiovascular endurance, boosting strength, or preserving overall well-being, trainers can assist clients in utilizing fitness technology to foster autonomy and internal drive. Professionals ought to discourage excessive emphasis on appearance-based metrics, as they frequently lead to social physique anxiety (Zartaloudi et al., 2023), and steer clients toward performance-oriented objectives that highlight skill enhancement and long-term health.

Fitness professionals could also find value in informing clients about the psychological impacts of social comparison (Crusius et al., 2022) and the significance of prioritizing personal development. Trainers can assist clients in making informed decisions on engaging with fitness technology by elucidating how social features may induce anxiety and dissatisfaction (Zartaloudi et al., 2023). Moreover, trainers have the option to motivate clients to utilize functionalities such as private progress tracking or achievement logging, enabling introspection free from public evaluation. Offering tools for mental wellness, like breathing exercises, affirmations, and mindfulness techniques, could assist clients in dealing with anxiety and promoting a positive mindset in their pursuit of fitness.

Best Practices for Developers: Designing User-Centered, Supportive Platforms

To developers, comprehending the psychological impacts of fitness technology can guide design choices that emphasize users' mental and physical health (Limone & Toto, 2022). The data suggests that social and competitive elements, although effective at increasing engagement, can also cultivate environments of social comparison and anxiety. Developers can foster platforms that facilitate healthier relationships with fitness technology by implementing a user-centered approach focused on personal growth (Zartaloudi et al., 2023).

One suggestion is that developers should prioritize features that highlight personal achievements and progress monitoring instead of social status (Woessner et al., 2021). For example, instead of emphasizing leaderboards, applications could include personal progress charts, goal completion badges, and notifications for personal bests to motivate users to celebrate their accomplishments individually. Personalized cues, such as reminders to ponder recent achievements or prompts to establish goals unrelated to appearance, could assist users in more conscientious interaction with the technology (Ryan & Deci, 2020). Revised: Customizable privacy options enable users to manage the metrics they disclose publicly, aiding individuals who prioritize personal progress over external benchmarks (Limone & Toto, 2022).

Furthermore, developers may contemplate incorporating mental health resources into fitness technology to aid users dealing with social physique anxiety or body image issues (Zartaloudi et al., 2023). One way to support users is by providing optional guided mindfulness sessions, positive affirmation exercises, or personalized wellness tips. Another option is to enable users to schedule reminders for regular breaks from social or competitive functions, promoting a more balanced interaction (Limone & Toto, 2022). By considering mental health during the design process, developers can create platforms that improve physical health and support psychological well-being.

Creating a Balanced Approach: Integrating Technology, Well-Being, and Self-Awareness

The results of this study underscore the importance of a well-rounded strategy for fitness technology, which empowers users while safeguarding them from the adverse impacts of social comparison (Codina et al., 2024). Through utilizing fitness technology as a means for self-exploration rather than seeking social approval, individuals can develop a more robust and healthier self-concept. It is crucial for users striving to uphold a positive self-concept to establish intrinsic goals that prioritize well-being, engage mindfully with social aspects, and concentrate on personal accomplishments rather than external benchmarks (Crusius et al., 2022).

For those in the field of fitness, it is crucial to prioritize leading clients toward intrinsic motivation and self-compassion in their fitness endeavors (Oginni et al., 2024). Encouraging clients to prioritize personal growth and providing assistance in navigating social pressures can facilitate clients in making informed and psychologically supportive decisions when utilizing fitness technology (Limone & Toto, 2022). Trainers and coaches possess the ability to assist clients in comprehending the intricate impacts of fitness technology and offer methods for effectively utilizing these tools to enhance well-being.

Conclusion

This section has discussed approaches for engaging with fitness technology in a responsible manner, utilizing knowledge from theoretical models and practical studies (Codina et al., 2024). The potential of fitness technology to motivate self-improvement and development is noteworthy; however, its design and utilization must be handled with care. By emphasizing personal objectives, concentrating on internal drive (Ryan & Deci, 2020), and cultivating surroundings that reduce social comparisons (Crusius et al., 2022), individuals can maximize the advantages of fitness technology while protecting their psychological well-being.

This analysis yielded several important recommendations to mitigate the psychological effects of fitness technology. Platforms ought to prioritize personal growth over metrics that foster social comparison, guiding users to concentrate on their individual accomplishments (Zartaloudi et al., 2023). Furthermore, enhancing functions that promote intrinsic motivation and autonomy may cultivate a more positive connection with fitness technology by coinciding with users' individual objectives and principles (Deci & Ryan, 1985). Additionally, it is essential to incorporate personalized privacy configurations enabling users to exert more authority over their social sharing choices, thereby empowering them to regulate their presence on the platform (Codina et al., 2024). Additionally, the inclusion of mental health support and wellness resources could offer valuable aid to individuals experiencing social physique anxiety (Limone & Toto, 2022). Ultimately, educating fitness professionals to effectively assist clients in utilizing these technologies can aid in their ability to utilize the tools in a manner that enhances wellness and reduces stress (Oginni et al., 2024).

The success of these methods relies on the joint collaboration of users, experts, and developers in establishing and upholding conducive fitness tech settings (Ryan & Deci, 2020). Users must be empowered to make informed choices about their engagement with technology, while professionals need to stay informed about both the benefits and risks of various features. Developers have a duty to prioritize user well-being over engagement metrics (Woessner et al., 2021).

Looking ahead, the challenge lies in continuing to innovate while maintaining a focus on psychological safety and user well-being. As fitness technology advances, the principles discussed in this chapter can be utilized as a framework for developing more inclusive and effective tools that enhance users' fitness experiences (Limone & Toto, 2022). The future of fitness technology hinges on balancing the motivational advantages of tracking and social elements while safeguarding users' mental well-being and encouraging sustainable, self-driven fitness routines.

By integrating these balanced strategies, the fitness technology sector can transition toward a holistic framework that promotes both physical and mental wellness. This evolution will require ongoing evaluation and adjustment of current practices, but the potential benefits—in terms of both user satisfaction and long-term health outcomes—make this effort worthwhile (Codina et al., 2024). The future of fitness technology is not only about monitoring physical activity but also about promoting resilience, self-acceptance, and sustainable health habits for all individuals.

Chapter 7

THE BIGGER PICTURE—FITNESS TECHNOLOGY IN A DIGITAL WORLD

Expanding its perspective, this chapter places fitness technology in the context of the broader digital health movement, analyzing its social ramifications and ethical dilemmas. This chapter delves deeper into individual-level perspectives by examining the impact of fitness technology on social norms, attitudes toward health, and body image at a broader level, connecting the micro-level effects to larger societal trends.

The swift growth of fitness technology reflects a wider change in how people interact with health and wellness in the digital era (Woessner et al., 2021). As dedicated devices and apps for tracking, optimizing, and sharing fitness progress become more widespread, the impact of these technologies extends beyond individual fitness objectives to shape societal perspectives on health, body image, and self-esteem. This section contextualizes the outcomes of the research within the broader scope of digital health, delving into the societal implications of fitness technology, its correlation with mental health, and the ethical and psychological factors that emerge as fitness technology is increasingly incorporated into everyday routines (Limone & Toto, 2022). Furthermore, it delves into potential paths for future research, pinpointing areas where additional investigation can enhance a more detailed comprehension of the psychological impacts of digital health tools.

Fitness Technology and the Broader Digital Health Movement

The integration of fitness technology falls under the broader digital health initiative, comprising various tools and gadgets aimed at enhancing health outcomes, enhancing medical care availability, and promoting proactive self-care of physical and mental health (Oginni et al., 2024). With the promotion of digital health tools by governments, healthcare organizations, and technology companies, fitness technology has emerged as a prominent method to promote physical activity, weight management, and health awareness. Wearable devices, health monitoring apps, and online health platforms collectively support the expanding digital health ecosystem, aiming to enable individuals to manage their health using easily accessible technology (Zartaloudi et al., 2023).

In this ecosystem, fitness technology has a distinct role in prioritizing preventive health (Woessner et al., 2021). Other digital health tools may focus on managing chronic conditions or offering telemedicine services, whereas fitness technology is centered on proactive health management, promoting the development of healthy habits prior to the need for medical intervention. Fitness technology plays a significant role for numerous users by serving as a daily prompt of their health objectives, promoting accountability and strengthening a dedication to well-being. However, this study demonstrates that while fitness technology provides motivational advantages, it can also lead to unintended psychological outcomes such as social comparison and anxiety (Zartaloudi et al., 2023). This dual effect underscores the necessity for a harmonized strategy in the realm of digital health, merging the emphasis on physical wellness with the recognition of mental well-being.

The Social Influence of Fitness Technology on Body Image

Fitness technology's impact goes beyond individual users to influence societal perspectives on body image, fitness standards, and self-esteem (Zartaloudi et al., 2023). With the growing trend of individuals sharing their fitness progress and routines on social media, fitness technology has emerged as a key factor in fostering comparisons based on appearance and shaping body image standards. The results of this study indicate that the visibility of others' fitness journeys can result in social physique anxiety and increased self-awareness in certain individuals, particularly when their own achievements do not align with the ideals set by peers or fitness influencers (Crusius et al., 2022).

Sociocultural theories propose that exposure to idealized body types in media may result in internalizing societal beauty norms, leading to body dissatisfaction and self-esteem challenges (Oginni et al., 2024). The extensive dissemination of fitness accomplishments on social media platforms enhances this phenomenon, exposing users to both images of fitness triumph and quantifiable measures of physical success (Limone & Toto, 2022). Upon witnessing peers achieve specific milestones, such as hitting a desired weight or undergoing a noticeable transformation, individuals might sense an obligation to replicate such outcomes, even if they are impractical or unachievable in their own situations. The process of comparing oneself and self-assessment in a digital setting results in a scenario where self-esteem is closely linked to physical attributes, often leading to negative impacts on mental well-being and self-approval (Festinger, 1954).

Fitness Technology and Mental Health: Dual Impacts and Considerations

The correlation between fitness technology and mental well-being is intricate, presenting advantages and drawbacks. On the one hand, fitness technology encourages physical activity, a practice known to positively impact mental health by alleviating symptoms of anxiety, depression, and stress (Codina et al., 2024). Regular physical activity, combined with fitness monitoring and goal-setting functions, has been proven to increase endorphin levels, enhance sleep quality, and elevate mood, thereby establishing a beneficial cycle that promotes general well-being. For individuals who view fitness technology as a means for personal development, these mental health advantages are especially evident, as they derive physical and psychological benefits from their interaction with the technology (Ryan & Deci, 2020).

Nevertheless, as indicated by this study, fitness technology may bring about mental health difficulties, especially for individuals susceptible to social comparison, body dissatisfaction, or performance-related anxiety (Zartaloudi et al., 2023). The display of peer accomplishments, the expectations to conform to external criteria, and the emphasis on numerical measures may alter individuals' incentives from inherent pleasure in physical activity to seeking external approval (Limone & Toto, 2022). This transition can result in heightened stress, lowered self-worth, and feelings of inadequacy for certain individuals as they strive to achieve goals that seem more challenging. This dual impact highlights the significance of developing fitness technology that enhances both physical health and mental well-being, prioritizing personal advancement over rivalry and cultivating a favorable, encouraging user interaction (Oginni et al., 2024).

Future Directions for Research on Fitness Technology and Psychological Well-Being

With the ongoing evolution of fitness technology, additional research is crucial to enhance our comprehension of its psychological effects and to establish methods that encourage beneficial involvement (Woessner et al., 2021). Various areas necessitate further investigation, especially with regards to the impact of diverse demographics, personality traits, and usage patterns on users' reactions to fitness technology. Comprehending these differences can guide specific interventions, allowing users to utilize fitness technology in a manner that corresponds to their individual requirements and mental health objectives (Zartaloudi et al., 2023).

An area with promising potential for future study involves investigating the impact of fitness technology on various age groups and demographics (Limone & Toto, 2022). Subsequent research could explore the perspectives of younger age groups, such as adolescents, who are particularly susceptible to issues related to social comparison and body image. Likewise, it is possible for research to investigate the experiences of female users, whose body image concerns may vary as a result of gender-specific societal pressures (Codina et al., 2024). Studying the interaction of these groups with fitness technology and its effects on their self-perception, drive, and psychological well-being could offer valuable insights into the unique requirements of each group.

These discoveries may guide the development of features that address social body image issues and encourage a variety of fitness environments.

Another research avenue worth exploring is the impact of personality traits on users' reactions to fitness technology (Crusius et al., 2022). Individual interactions with social features and responses to metrics may be influenced by personality traits like competitiveness, perfectionism, and self-esteem. For example, individuals with elevated levels of competitiveness may experience increased levels of stress or anxiety when faced with social comparison, while those with high self-esteem may be less influenced by external validation pressures (Zartaloudi et al., 2023). Through the analysis of these personality-driven reactions, researchers can pinpoint potential risk factors and formulate suggestions for users to interact with fitness technology in a manner that enhances their mental health.

Longitudinal research is necessary to comprehend the enduring psychological impacts of utilizing fitness technology (Codina et al., 2024). Although this research provides valuable information on users' immediate experiences, longitudinal studies could elucidate the effects of prolonged engagement with fitness technology on self-concept, body image, and mental health. Such research could provide a more comprehensive view of fitness technology's psychological impact, highlighting patterns of resilience, adaptation, or vulnerability (Zartaloudi et al., 2023).

Ethical Considerations and the Responsibility of Developers

The results of this study bring to light significant ethical inquiries regarding the development and marketing of fitness technology (Woessner et al., 2021). Developers have a responsibility to contemplate the potential mental health effects of their products, as they craft tools that significantly shape users' views on health and self-esteem. Recommending platforms that promote users to establish attainable, internal objectives rather than emphasizing external approval is crucial for fostering users' comprehensive well-being (Ryan & Deci, 2020). Developers should take into account the risks linked to social comparison and create functionalities that foster personal development, providing alternatives for private goal monitoring and personalized feedback instead of public rankings (Zartaloudi et al., 2023).

Ethical design encompasses being transparent about the utilization and sharing of data (Limone & Toto, 2022). Users should be made aware of how their data influences their experience in fitness technology, especially when shared on public platforms. Developers can empower users to pursue their health goals by prioritizing user privacy and mental health, creating platforms that are both motivating and psychologically supportive (Codina et al., 2024).

Conclusion

Fitness technology is not only transforming individual fitness experiences but also influencing societal perspectives on health, body image, and self-esteem (Codina et al., 2024). The findings of this study emphasize the importance of a holistic approach that values both physical and mental well-being when it comes to the dual effects of fitness technology on motivation and anxiety (Zartaloudi et al., 2023). By comprehending the wider social and psychological consequences of fitness technology, users, professionals, and developers can collaborate to establish healthier digital health ecosystems.

The future of fitness technology necessitates careful consideration of various key areas to promote user well-being and inclusivity. It will be crucial to integrate mental health support with physical fitness tracking to recognize the interconnectedness of mental and physical well-being (Oginni et al., 2024). Moreover, the implementation of functionalities that mitigate the risk of negative social comparisons can enhance user experience in a more positive manner (Crusius et al., 2022). Ensuring user privacy and data security is of utmost importance, enabling users to interact with these platforms without worries about data misuse or breaches (Ryan & Deci, 2020). It is crucial to promote inclusive and diverse depictions of health and fitness to ensure that all individuals feel acknowledged and validated in their distinct fitness paths (Zartaloudi et al., 2023). Placing importance on cultivating intrinsic motivation rather than external validation can redirect users' attention toward personal development and self-realization instead of seeking validation from others (Ryan & Deci, 2020). These factors collectively contribute to establishing a future in fitness technology that is more balanced and supportive.

As the field of fitness technology progresses, continual research and ethical deliberation are crucial for managing its impact on individuals and society. Future research can elucidate demographic variances, personality traits, and enduring impacts, offering valuable insights for the development of user-centric, ethical designs (Crusius et al., 2022). By cultivating a culture of self-acceptance and individual development, fitness technology has the capacity to promote not just physical fitness, but also resilience, self-compassion, and comprehensive well-being in the digital era.

The future challenge involves balancing technological progress with mental health considerations to ensure that fitness technology advancements improve rather than harm users' well-being. Through ongoing research, deliberate design, and ethical deployment, fitness technology has the potential to advance its primary objective: assisting users in their pursuit of holistic health and well-being (Woessner et al., 2021).

Chapter 8

KEY FINDINGS AND IMPLICATIONS

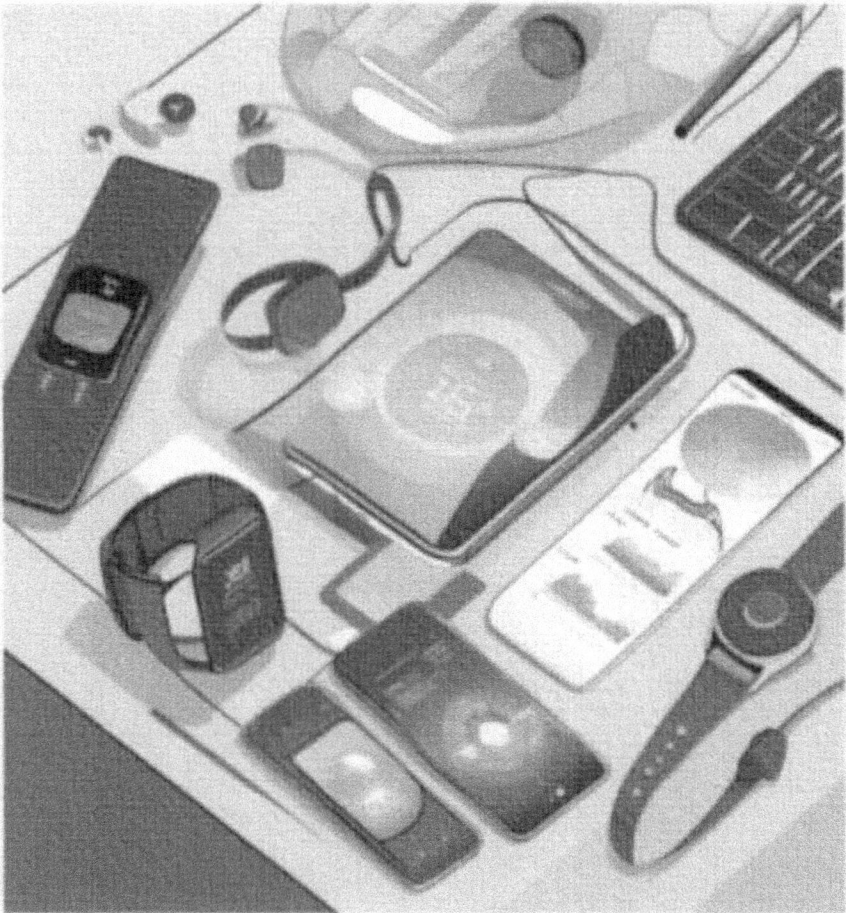

By conducting a thorough examination of empirical data, this chapter integrates the quantitative and qualitative findings, establishing links between psychological theories and observed results. This chapter serves as a connection between theoretical insights and practical findings, emphasizing essential points for stakeholders and setting the stage for the final reflection on the broader implications of fitness technology.

Introduction to Key Findings

The chapter offers a thorough examination of the research results, integrating both quantitative and qualitative data to offer a comprehensive insight into the impact of fitness technology on psychological well-being (Codina et al., 2024). As discussed in earlier sections, fitness technology has a twofold influence: it can inspire individuals and enhance their physical self-perception, yet it also brings about the potential for social comparison and heightened social physique anxiety (Zartaloudi et al., 2023). The discoveries detailed in this chapter emphasize the intricate nature of the topic, elucidating the various ways in which different aspects of fitness technology impact positive and negative results. Drawing from Social Comparison Theory (Festinger, 1954; Crusius et al., 2022), Self-Determination Theory (Ryan & Deci, 2020), and the Hierarchical Model of Physical Self-Concept (Marsh, 1996), this book interprets these findings within broader psychological frameworks to illuminate their implications for users, fitness professionals, and developers alike.

Quantitative Findings

The quantitative aspect of this research entailed the examination of data from the Physical Self-Description Inventory (PSDI) and Social Physique

Table 1 Descriptive statistics of key variables.

Variable	Mean	Standard Deviation	Min	Max	Frequency of High Scores (%)
Physical Self-Concept	4.3	0.9	2.0	6.0	55
Social Physique Anxiety	3.8	1.1	1.5	6.5	48
Frequency of Technology Use	4.7	1.0	3.0	7.0	62
Engagement with Social Features	3.9	1.2	2.0	6.0	53

Anxiety Scale (SPAS), alongside self-reported technology utilization metrics. Through the analysis of correlations and regression outcomes, we acquire understanding of the quantifiable connections between the utilization of fitness technology and psychological aspects, notably physical self-concept and social physique anxiety (Marsh, 1996).

Descriptive Statistics

The descriptive statistics offer a summary of the participants' scores on the PSDI and SPAS, along with the frequency and intensity of fitness technology usage as detailed by Zartaloudi et al. (2023). The preliminary data sets the stage for further examination, enabling us to identify overarching patterns in users' self-perception and anxiety levels. Table 1 presents an overview of these results, outlining the averages, standard deviations, and occurrence distributions for every variable.

The mean self-perception score of 4.3 indicates a moderately favorable self-image among respondents, with a majority (55 percent) scoring high in this domain (Marsh, 1996). This discovery suggests that fitness technology helps many users feel competent and physically capable, enhancing the motivational elements highlighted in earlier sections (Ryan & Deci, 2020). Conversely, the average score for social physique anxiety, at 3.8, indicates a substantial number of individuals facing moderate to high levels of anxiety linked to their physical appearance (Zartaloudi et al., 2023). Nearly half of the participants (48 percent) achieved scores above the midpoint in social physique anxiety, indicating the influence of social comparison aspects on body image worries.

Valuable insights can also be obtained from the frequency of technology use and engagement with social features (Woessner et al., 2021). The score of 4.7 indicates active engagement with fitness technology, while the score of

Table 2 Correlation coefficients between key variables.

Variables	Physical Self-Concept	Social Physique Anxiety	Frequency of Technology Use	Engagement with Social Features
Physical Self-Concept	1.0	−0.45*	0.53*	0.48*
Social Physique Anxiety	−0.45*	1.0	0.42*	0.63**
Frequency of Technology Use	0.53*	0.42*	1.0	0.59*
Engagement with Social Features	0.48*	0.63**	0.59*	1.0

Note. $*p < 0.05$, $**p < 0.01$

3.9 suggests moderate interaction with social features. The data highlights the dual engagement patterns discovered in this study, indicating that users are attracted to fitness technology for self-enhancement, while also engaging with functions that encourage social comparison, impacting motivation and anxiety (Crusius et al., 2022).

Correlational Analysis

The correlational analysis enhances understanding of the connections among fitness technology use, physical self-concept, and social physique anxiety. Table 2 displays the correlation coefficients for important variables, emphasizing significant associations that enhance our comprehension of the influence of fitness technology on psychological outcomes.

The analysis indicates a positive correlation between the frequency of technology utilization and physical self-concept ($r = 0.53$, $p < 0.05$), implying that increased interaction with fitness technology is linked to improved perceptions of physical self-worth (Codina et al., 2024). This finding affirms the idea that fitness technology enhances self-efficacy through continuous feedback and measurable advancements, consistent with the Self-Determination Theory's focus on competence as a motivator (Ryan & Deci, 2020).

On the other hand, a statistically significant positive relationship exists between social feature engagement and social physique anxiety ($r = 0.63$, $p < 0.01$) (Zartaloudi et al., 2023). This discovery indicates that individuals who regularly interact with the social and comparative features of fitness technology may be prone to feeling anxious about how others perceive their bodies. The robust relationship between these variables lends support to the utilization of Social Comparison Theory (Festinger, 1954), as individuals who engage in frequent comparisons of their accomplishments with others tend to exhibit elevated levels of body-related anxiety (Crusius et al., 2022).

The inverse relationship observed between physical self-concept and social physique anxiety ($r = -0.45$, $p < 0.05$) suggests that elevated self-concept correlates with reduced anxiety levels, indicating a shielding influence of self-efficacy (Marsh, 1996). Individuals with a strong perception of physical self-worth may exhibit greater resilience toward adverse impacts of social comparison by attributing their accomplishments as intrinsic rather than comparative to others (Zartaloudi et al., 2023).

Regression Analysis

The regression analysis performed in this study provides additional understanding of the predictive connections among fitness technology use, physical

Table 3 Regression analysis: Predictors of physical self-concept and social physique anxiety.

Predictor Variables	Dependent Variable	β (Beta)	p-value	R²
Frequency of Technology Use	Physical Self-Concept	0.41	< 0.05	0.29
Engagement with Social Features	Physical Self-Concept	0.32	< 0.05	
Frequency of Technology Use	Social Physique Anxiety	0.38	< 0.01	0.42
Engagement with Social Features	Social Physique Anxiety	0.57	< 0.01	

self-concept, and social physique anxiety (Codina et al., 2024). Through the analysis of these predictors, we pinpoint the factors most strongly linked to enhanced self-concept or elevated anxiety, offering a detailed insight into the ways in which fitness technology influences users' psychological welfare.

The regression analysis indicates that both the frequency of technology use and engagement with social features are significant predictors of physical self-concept and social physique anxiety, albeit in varying degrees (Zartaloudi et al., 2023). Regarding physical self-concept, the frequency of technology use is the most significant predictor ($\beta = 0.41$, $p < 0.05$), indicating that consistent interaction with fitness technology enhances users' self-perceptions (Ryan & Deci, 2020). In accordance with the descriptive and correlational results, this supports the notion that providing feedback on personal progress can boost users' feelings of competence and self-esteem, ultimately reinforcing their physical self-perception.

Notably, involvement with social aspects is also a notable, albeit slightly less powerful, indicator of physical self-perception ($\beta = 0.32$, $p < 0.05$) (Limone & Toto, 2022). This discovery suggests that the social elements of fitness technology may enhance self-perception by fostering a sense of community or validation upon goal achievement. Nevertheless, this phenomenon seems to have a more intricate nature, since the variable (engagement with social features) also strongly predicts social physique anxiety ($\beta = 0.57$, $p < 0.01$) (Marsh, 1996).

The social physique anxiety model indicates that interaction with social aspects is a stronger indicator than the frequency of technology usage (Zartaloudi et al., 2023). This indicates that users' anxiety is primarily linked to the social and comparative aspects of fitness technology rather than the technology use per se. According to Crusius et al. (2022), individuals who actively participate in social sharing, seek leaderboard rankings, and engage in competitive challenges are prone to experiencing elevated body-related anxiety. Accordingly, this aligns with the assertion of Social Comparison Theory that comparisons in appearance-related contexts can reduce self-esteem and increase social anxiety.

The R^2 values of the regression models (0.29 for physical self-concept and 0.42 for social physique anxiety) suggest that the predictors account for a significant portion of the variance in each dependent variable. However, it should be noted that other variables not addressed in this research could impact these findings (Marsh, 1996). This paves the way for future studies to investigate other factors, like personality traits or demographic variances, that might influence the correlation between the utilization of fitness technology and mental well-being.

Qualitative Findings with Thematic Analysis

The qualitative aspect of this research enhances the quantitative results by offering detailed insights into users' subjective experiences (Codina et al., 2024). Through thematic analysis, three central themes were discerned: (1) Technology as a Motivator; (2) Social Comparison and Anxiety; and (3) Enhanced Self-Awareness and Physical Self-Concept.

Each theme is elaborated upon below, with participant quotes providing insight into the intricate impacts of fitness technology on users' mental and emotional reactions (Limone & Toto, 2022).

Theme 1: Technology as a motivator

The concept of Technology as a Motivator was a prominent theme in the narratives of participants, as numerous users detailed how fitness technology assisted them in sustaining consistency, establishing attainable objectives, and acknowledging progress (Ryan & Deci, 2020). The inclusion of features like step counts, distance trackers, and daily performance summaries motivated these users to overcome both physical and psychological obstacles (Oginni et al., 2024). Numerous individuals emphasized the motivational influence of establishing personalized goals within the application, detailing how these characteristics changed physical activity from a task into a gratifying endeavor.

A participant articulated, "Observing my progress visually serves as a source of motivation for me." This statement demonstrates how fitness technology supports a growth mindset by enabling users to concentrate on gradual progress rather than instant outcomes (Ryan & Deci, 2020). For individuals who view fitness technology as a means for personal growth, the feedback they obtain boosts self-efficacy and feelings of achievement, aligning with Self-Determination Theory's focus on competence in maintaining intrinsic motivation (Codina et al., 2024).

Theme 2: Social comparison and anxiety

The second theme, Social Comparison and Anxiety, highlights the more complex elements of fitness technology, particularly for users who interact with social functions such as leaderboards, progress photos, and community challenges (Zartaloudi et al., 2023). The social elements posed a dual challenge for numerous participants, serving as both a source of motivation and exacerbating feelings of inadequacy, self-consciousness, and social physique anxiety. Individuals who regularly monitored their rankings in community leaderboards or compared their performance to that of friends and online influencers reported feeling body-related anxiety and facing expectations to adhere to specific fitness standards (Crusius et al., 2022).

A participant expressed difficulty in comparing oneself to others who are more advanced. This quotation highlights the mental pressure caused by comparing oneself to others in social settings, especially in fitness environments where looks and abilities are greatly emphasized (Festinger, 1954). For these individuals, the social dimension of fitness technology cultivated a competitive environment rather than a sense of community, linking self-esteem to others' views and accomplishments (Ryan & Deci, 2020).

Theme 3: Enhanced self-awareness and physical self-concept

The concluding theme, Enhanced Self-Awareness and Physical Self-Concept, emphasizes the beneficial psychological effects of fitness technology on individuals who interact with it for self-examination and personal growth (Marsh, 1996). Participants articulated that consistent monitoring of their progress resulted in heightened self-awareness, facilitating a deeper comprehension of their physical abilities and constraints. Fitness technology functioned as a reflective tool for these users, offering unbiased insights to assist in aligning fitness aspirations with practical expectations and personal beliefs (Codina et al., 2024).

A participant expressed that monitoring their progress has enhanced their understanding of their capabilities. The process of self-reflection enhances one's physical self-concept by providing insight into strengths and areas for development (Crusius et al., 2022). For these individuals, fitness technology offered a feeling of empowerment, enabling them to mold their self-image through their accomplishments rather than conforming to societal ideals of fitness or attractiveness (Limone & Toto, 2022).

Theoretical Context and Practical Implications

The results closely correspond with well-known psychological theories, offering a glimpse into the impact of fitness technology on motivation, self-concept, and social physique anxiety (Ryan & Deci, 2020). These findings hold crucial significance for different stakeholders. Users are emphasized methods to utilize fitness technology that support mental well-being and reduce anxiety levels (Zartaloudi et al., 2023). Developers are urged to design features that promote intrinsic motivation and mitigate influences of social comparison (Woessner et al., 2021). Fitness professionals have the potential to assist clients in adopting healthier technology habits (Oginni et al., 2024), while researchers are urged to pinpoint avenues for additional exploration (Codina et al., 2024).

In order to enhance fitness technology, various essential suggestions have been identified: placing emphasis on personal progress tracking rather than social comparison features, integrating customizable privacy settings, designing features that bolster intrinsic motivation, offering tools for mental health support and self-reflection, and delivering guidance on healthy technology use. These observations aid in the comprehension of the potential design of fitness technology to enhance both physical and psychological well-being (Crusius et al., 2022). The main task ahead is to apply these discoveries in a manner that encourages sustainable health practices while protecting users' mental well-being (Zartaloudi et al., 2023).

Conclusions and Future Directions

The exhaustive examination of quantitative and qualitative data uncovers significant patterns crucial for future research and development of fitness technology (Codina et al., 2024). One significant pattern to note is the dual effect of these platforms, with personal growth enhancing motivation and self-efficacy (Ryan & Deci, 2020), while social comparison mechanisms may result in unfavorable consequences, influenced by individual variances and usage habits (Crusius et al., 2022). Moreover, essential moderating elements, like personality traits, usage habits, feature preferences, and modes of social support and community involvement, impact how individuals engage with fitness technology (Woessner et al., 2021).

Future research directions highlighted by these findings include longitudinal studies to explore the enduring psychological consequences of utilizing fitness technology, cross-cultural analyses to elucidate divergent influence mechanisms, and inquiries into protective elements against social physique anxiety. Exploring the impact of specific platform features on various demographic groups and developing mental health-focused features are potential areas for future research according to Oginni et al. (2024). The practical implications of this analysis involve creating personalized feature sets tailored to user characteristics, integrating mental health screening tools, developing educational materials for promoting healthy technology usage, and designing features that prioritize intrinsic motivation and privacy-oriented tracking options (Codina et al., 2024).

In relation to theoretical implications, this study broadens current frameworks by enhancing the comprehension of social comparison in digital settings (Festinger, 1954), aiding the implementation of Self-Determination Theory in technological landscapes (Ryan & Deci, 2020), and progressing understanding of physical self-concept development (Marsh, 1996). These findings emphasize the importance of developing fitness technology that promotes both physical and mental wellness, encouraging lasting and positive user involvement.

Chapter 9

CONCLUSION—TOWARD A BALANCED FUTURE IN FITNESS TECHNOLOGY

This chapter highlights the ethical responsibilities of developers, fitness professionals, and policymakers in the development of user-centric fitness technology. This chapter underscores the significance of user privacy, ethical data usage, and the development of technology that reduces social comparison, setting the stage for the aspirational future of fitness technology in the concluding chapter.

Summary of Key Insights

The research has shed light on the dual effects of fitness technology on users' mental well-being, encompassing both its empowering capabilities and the psychological susceptibilities it may bring about (Codina et al., 2024). The research results indicate that fitness technology is a valuable instrument for self-enhancement. It promotes physical self-awareness and drive through organized feedback, goal setting, and community involvement. Through enhancing users' feelings of competence and promoting autonomy, fitness technology is in accordance with the tenets of Self-Determination Theory, proving to be a potent incentive for individuals pursuing fitness-related personal development (Ryan & Deci, 2020).

The study also underscores the dangers linked to social comparison, especially through functions that promote competitive or appearance-oriented engagements (Crusius et al., 2022). The data indicates a statistically significant relationship between interaction with social features and social physique anxiety. According to Zartaloudi et al. (2023), the competitive aspects of fitness technology may create environments in which self-esteem depends on external evaluations. Fitness technology could potentially lead to body dissatisfaction and a shift from intrinsic motivation to external validation for individuals sensitive to appearance-based pressures (Limone & Toto, 2022).

Further enhancement of understanding is achieved through qualitative findings, which unveil the subjective experiences underlying these trends. Participants conveyed gratitude for the motivational framework offered by fitness technology, while also expressing discontent over the expectation to adhere to idealized fitness standards (Codina et al., 2024). The narratives emphasize that the development of fitness technology should be based on principles that consider the intricate psychological terrain users navigate. Fitness technology serves as both a means of self-empowerment and a possible stress factor.

Addressing Limitations of the Study

Although the study findings provide valuable insights, it is important to consider several limitations when interpreting the results. The constraints pertain to the sample makeup, the extent of data gathering, and possible confounding factors, all of which impact the applicability and thoroughness of the findings (Zartaloudi et al., 2023).

Initially, the research included a sample of 40 male participants aged between 18 and 40, mainly sourced from gyms and fitness centers. Although this sample offers a preliminary insight into the influence of fitness technology, it restricts the generalizability of the study to wider demographics like women, older individuals, or those participating in fitness outside conventional gym settings (Limone & Toto, 2022). Research findings suggest that women may experience social physique anxiety and body image concerns differently as a result of unique societal pressures (Zartaloudi et al., 2023), indicating the potential for gender-inclusive research to uncover further insights.

Another constraint involves depending on self-reported data for technology usage and psychological evaluations. Self-reported measures can be biased, as participants might inadvertently exaggerate or underestimate their interaction with fitness technology or their anxiety levels (Woessner et al., 2021). Psychometric scales such as the PSDI (Marsh, 1996) and SPAS provide validated insights. Using objective usage data from fitness devices and apps would enhance the study's validity. Moreover, longitudinal data may offer insights into the enduring psychological impacts of fitness technology, elucidating whether users' encounters with social comparison and motivation evolve during prolonged engagement (Codina et al., 2024).

The research did not consider personality traits, such as competitiveness or self-esteem, which could influence how individuals react to social aspects in fitness technology (Crusius et al., 2022). Personality traits may play a role in users' perception and reaction to social comparison, as competitive individuals might feel more motivated and anxious when faced with leaderboards and rankings. Future research endeavors may be enhanced by incorporating personality evaluations to gain a deeper insight into how individual variations influence the psychological effects of fitness technology (Woessner et al., 2021).

Future Directions for Research and Practice

The results and constraints of this study indicate numerous opportunities for future investigation and practical implementation. The advancement of fitness technology underscores the importance of exploring these areas for creating tools that promote overall well-being.

Research recommendations

Future investigations ought to delve into the experiences of various demographic groups, such as women, adolescents, and older individuals

(Limone & Toto, 2022). Body image concerns and social comparison tendencies may differ significantly among demographic groups, and recognizing these variances could assist in developing more inclusive fitness technologies. For instance, an examination of the influence of fitness technology on adolescents, who are especially susceptible to social comparison (Crusius et al., 2022), may provide a deeper understanding of features suitable for their age that promote self-esteem rather than appearance-based stressors (Oginni et al., 2024).

Analyzing personality characteristics, as previously stated, would enhance the complexity of forthcoming research. Researchers could pinpoint predictors of social physique anxiety and motivation toward fitness technology by analyzing factors such as competitiveness, perfectionism, and self-esteem (Zartaloudi et al., 2023). This comprehension could lead to customized suggestions for technology usage, ensuring that individuals interact with these resources in a manner that supports their mental health.

Long-term research is essential for comprehending the progression of users' interaction with fitness technology over time (Codina et al., 2024). Over the course of several months or years, monitoring shifts in self-perception, drive, and anxiety related to physical appearance could unveil trends in adjustment, strength, or susceptibility, aiding in the enhancement of optimal strategies for utilizing fitness technology. Furthermore, cross-cultural studies may explore the impact of societal norms and cultural attitudes on users' reactions to fitness technology (Oginni et al., 2024).

Practical innovations for developers and fitness professionals

Developers have the capability to incorporate mental health aspects into fitness technology, thus establishing platforms that cater to both physical and psychological well-being (Woessner et al., 2021). Developers can diminish the focus on social comparison by creating features that promote users to establish personal goals and track their progress confidentially. Customizable features enabling users to regulate the aspects of their progress shared publicly would enable users to make decisions that support their mental well-being (Ryan & Deci, 2020).

Another potential area for improvement involves incorporating mental health resources into fitness apps. Optional mindfulness exercises, positive affirmations, or self-reflection prompts may assist users in developing a well-rounded approach to fitness, highlighting self-compassion in addition to physical accomplishments (Limone & Toto, 2022). Developers have the option to consider integrating reminders that encourage users to reflect on personal goals, commemorate achievements, and prevent burnout. These characteristics would cultivate an environment conducive to growth that promotes internal motivation, enabling users to enjoy the psychological advantages of fitness technology while avoiding the pitfalls of social comparison (Ryan & Deci, 2020).

The study emphasizes the significance of fitness professionals educating clients on the psychological impacts of fitness technology (Codina et al., 2024). Trainers and coaches play a vital role in assisting clients in setting personal growth-oriented goals, steering them toward prioritizing functional performance rather than appearance-based results. Fitness professionals have the ability to cultivate healthier relationships with technology for their clients by highlighting fitness as a personal journey and discouraging an excessive focus on competitive metrics (Crusius et al., 2022).

Vision for the Future of Fitness Technology

The capacity of fitness technology to enhance both physical and mental well-being is significant (Woessner et al., 2021). With the growing integration of digital health tools into everyday life, this study emphasizes the significance of a balanced, user-centric strategy that places emphasis on well-being rather than external approval. Fitness technology possesses the ability to encourage self-enhancement, perseverance, and self-approval, but only through intentional design and application (Zartaloudi et al., 2023).

In the future, the advancement of fitness technology should focus on specific key areas to improve user support and enhance the overall experience. In order to ensure that individuals from various backgrounds and abilities can interact with these platforms without obstacles, it is essential that inclusivity and accessibility are prioritized (Codina et al., 2024). Furthermore, fostering psychological safety and providing support can enhance users' sense of security and empathy, meeting mental health needs in the fitness technology sphere (Limone & Toto, 2022). Individual autonomy and customization are crucial, as they enable people to customize their experiences according to their specific objectives and principles (Ryan & Deci, 2020). The integration of evidence-based design practices can enhance the refinement of these tools to better cater to user needs through reliable research (Codina et al., 2024). Safeguarding user trust and ensuring the integrity and transparency of their information are crucial aspects of ethical data handling and privacy protection (Woessner et al., 2021). Collectively, these priorities lay the groundwork for a future in fitness technology that is more supportive, inclusive, and secure.

Through understanding the intricate psychological aspects of social comparison and motivation, a collaborative effort among developers, experts, and users can be made to establish a fitness setting that enables individuals to strive toward their health objectives while safeguarding their mental well-being (Crusius et al., 2022). The future of fitness technology hinges on its capacity to holistically aid users, fostering physical fitness along with resilience, self-compassion, and a positive self-perception.

Concluding Remarks

The development of fitness technology signifies a crucial point where digital advancement and human welfare meet (Woessner et al., 2021). The results of this study illustrate that technology can greatly boost motivation and assist in achieving physical health objectives, but its psychological effects must be carefully evaluated. Moving forward, the challenge remains in developing technological solutions that utilize digital tracking and community support advantages, while safeguarding users from the possible adverse impacts of social comparison and external validation (Codina et al., 2024).

The issues related to comparing and seeking validation in fitness technology highlight important lessons for future progress. Firstly, personalized strategies must be implemented to consider individual variations in motivation and susceptibility to social comparison, ensuring that functionalities align with a range of user encounters (Crusius et al., 2022). It is crucial to develop characteristics that prioritize intrinsic motivation rather than external validation, as it aids in users' internal objectives and overall welfare (Ryan & Deci, 2020). Moreover, the inclusion of mental health resources on fitness platforms can offer users essential tools to address their well-being in conjunction with physical health objectives (Limone & Toto, 2022). It is essential to prioritize privacy controls and user autonomy, enabling users to have more control over their interactions with features and the sharing of their progress (Zartaloudi et al., 2023). The utilization of evidence-based design methodologies may improve psychological support in fitness technology, establishing features on solid research and user-centered principles (Zartaloudi et al., 2023).

Success in advancing fitness technology hinges on continuous collaboration across multiple disciplines. Researchers are crucial in examining the enduring psychological effects, offering guidance for more empathetic design decisions (Woessner et al., 2021). Developers are required to persist in developing intricate, supportive functionalities that address users' mental and physical health requirements (Oginni et al., 2024). Mental health professionals can offer their expertise to ensure that these platforms promote psychological well-being, while fitness professionals can lead users toward healthy technology habits. Users play a crucial role as collaborators by providing feedback on their experiences and needs, influencing the future of fitness technology.

As we progress, the priority should be on creating technology that enriches rather than detracts from the human experience of health and wellness. The advancement of fitness technology hinges on more than just monitoring physical activity; it also involves assisting users in reaching their health goals and enhancing their mental well-being (Woessner et al., 2021). Through ongoing research, deliberate design, and dedication to user welfare, fitness technology has the potential to advance in order to effectively fulfill its primary objective: promoting holistic health and enduring lifestyle modifications for all individuals.

Chapter 10

FINAL REMARKS PART 1

Commencing the final chapter, Part 1 of Chapter 10 integrates the fundamental understandings from preceding chapters, amalgamating the primary discoveries on the dual psychological effects of fitness technology. This portion of the book examines the evidence and theories previously discussed, offering a comprehensive analysis on how fitness technology impacts users' psychological well-being. By grounding these reflections in Social Comparison Theory, Self-Determination Theory, and the Hierarchical Model of Physical Self-Concept, Part 1 establishes the groundwork for examining wider repercussions in Part 2.

Revisiting the Core Themes in Fitness Technology and Well-Being

In the course of this book, the research outcomes demonstrate the significant dual influence of fitness technology on the physical and psychological well-being of users (Codina et al., 2024). The advancement of fitness technology has revolutionized individual health routines by offering individuals resources for enhancing themselves, staying motivated, and monitoring progress. The utilization of fitness apps and wearable devices has resulted in a more robust physical self-perception, enhanced adherence to exercise schedules, and an increased feeling of accomplishment for numerous individuals. This form of positive feedback is consistent with the principles of Self-Determination Theory, emphasizing the significance of competence and autonomy in cultivating internal drive (Ryan & Deci, 2020).

Nevertheless, the research also underscores the unintentional outcomes that may result from functionalities that encourage social comparison, including leaderboards, community challenges, and appearance-based tracking (Crusius et al., 2022). Although designed to promote community and motivation, these factors can lead to an environment conducive to social physique anxiety. The findings indicated that individuals who regularly interacted with social aspects were prone to body image-related anxiety, as indicated by Zartaloudi et al. (2023), supporting the claim of Social Comparison Theory that comparing oneself to others can result in discontent, as proposed by Festinger (1954).

Essentially, fitness technology functions within a range encompassing motivation and anxiety, empowerment and vulnerability (Limone & Toto, 2022). Fitness technology is a potent tool for self-empowerment for individuals who focus on personal growth and private achievements through mindful engagement. For individuals who are prone to social comparison pressures, fitness technology has the potential to induce stress. The dual impact emphasizes the importance of a balanced approach, acknowledging both the advantages and psychological risks linked to fitness technology (Woessner et al., 2021).

Societal Implications of Fitness Technology in a Digital Health Context

The impact of fitness technology goes beyond individual users to influence broader cultural and societal perspectives on health, body image, and self-esteem (Limone & Toto, 2022). The rise in individuals sharing their fitness milestones, progress images, and exercise data on social platforms has led to a shift in societal discourse. Woessner et al. (2021) have discussed how health and physical well-being are not only personal goals but also indicators of success and commitment. This shift has significant implications for how society perceives health and wellness, as the visibility of fitness achievements encourages a normative ideal that values certain body types, appearances, and physical capabilities over others (Zartaloudi et al., 2023).

In the current digital health environment, fitness technology is frequently promoted as a means of personal empowerment, available to individuals of diverse fitness levels and backgrounds (Woessner et al., 2021). Nevertheless, the results of this study suggest that not all users perceive fitness technology as empowering; this insight suggests a need for more inclusive and balanced representations of health within fitness technology. Despite the importance of promoting physical health, digital health platforms must also consider mental well-being, acknowledging that the focus on fitness and body enhancement can result in adverse psychological effects (Ryan & Deci, 2020).

Fitness technology's role in the broader digital health movement underscores several essential priorities. Prioritizing accessibility and inclusivity in design is crucial to ensure that individuals from diverse backgrounds and abilities can utilize these platforms without encountering obstacles (Oginni et al., 2024). Equally crucial is the incorporation of functionalities that enhance psychological well-being, enabling users to participate with confidence while minimizing negative mental health impacts (Woessner et al., 2021). The consideration of cultural sensitivity in health promotion aims to align fitness technology with various communities, honoring their beliefs and customs (Crusius et al., 2022). Furthermore, it is crucial to strike a balance between motivation and well-being, ensuring that features are uplifting for users without jeopardizing their mental health. Ultimately, ethical considerations regarding data sharing and social features are essential as they safeguard user privacy and cultivate trust in the platform (Ryan & Deci, 2020). Collectively, these components demonstrate the increasing necessity for a deliberate, user-focused strategy to fitness technology in the realm of digital health.

Ethical Responsibilities of Stakeholders in Fitness Technology Development

As fitness technology increasingly impacts global health practices, ethical obligations should steer its advancement and utilization (Woessner et al., 2021). Given the study's results that emphasize the positive effects and psychological dangers of fitness technology, it is crucial for stakeholders such as developers, policymakers, and fitness experts to prioritize user well-being and implement a user-focused design and guidance strategy.

Developers have a crucial responsibility in influencing user experiences through the features they create, which directly affect user interactions with fitness technology (Codina et al., 2024). The study emphasizes the importance for developers to take into account mental health implications when incorporating social and competitive aspects. To illustrate, emphasizing characteristics that enable users to establish private objectives, monitor advancement regardless of public rankings, and participate in introspective activities can cultivate a more equitable and internal motivation (Ryan & Deci, 2020). The importance of transparency and data privacy is highlighted as crucial ethical factors (Limone & Toto, 2022). Developers must ensure the secure and transparent handling of users' personal health data as reliance on digital tools grows. Users must possess authority over their personal data to ensure autonomy and privacy (Woessner et al., 2021). Policymakers play a crucial role in setting industry standards that prioritize the psychological well-being of users (Oginni et al., 2024). Regulations promoting ethical design, transparency in data usage, and mental health safeguards can steer the industry toward practices that prioritize users. Policies focusing on the mental health implications linked to fitness technology are essential, especially for vulnerable groups like adolescents who could be highly impacted by social comparison pressures (Zartaloudi et al., 2023).

Fitness professionals are also responsible for educating and advising clients on the mindful use of fitness technology (Oginni et al., 2024). Trainers and coaches, regarded as reliable sources of fitness guidance, can assist clients in cultivating a positive interaction with digital resources through promoting self-set objectives, resilience, and self-kindness. Fitness professionals can promote intrinsic motivation instead of external validation to guide clients in utilizing technology in accordance with their mental health requirements (Codina et al., 2024).

Researchers enhance evidence-based practices in fitness technology. Through examining psychological effects, researchers can recognize risk and protective elements, guide forthcoming advancements, and evaluate lasting effects on welfare. Longitudinal and cross-cultural studies are particularly beneficial in comprehending the various impacts of fitness technology on users over time, aiding developers and policymakers in designing inclusive digital health tools (Limone & Toto, 2022).

Implications for Practice and Policy

The results of this study indicate various practical and policy implications that can assist in mitigating the dual effects of fitness technology on users' physical and psychological well-being. Developers, fitness professionals, policymakers, and researchers each play a part in promoting a balanced, user-centered approach to fitness technology.

Implications for developers

Developers are encouraged to prioritize the development of customizable features that enable users to personalize their fitness experiences based on individual goals and preferences (Woessner et al., 2021). By providing options for setting private milestones, disabling competitive elements, and opting out of social comparisons, users can be empowered to interact with fitness technology in a manner that prioritizes their mental well-being (Woessner et al., 2021). Ethical data management practices are essential, such as providing clear information about data use and empowering users to manage their personal information. This method upholds both privacy and autonomy (Zartaloudi et al., 2023).

Implications for fitness professionals

The results underscore the importance of fitness professionals educating clients on proper use of fitness technology. Trainers and coaches have the ability to assist clients in establishing achievable, performance-oriented objectives, comprehending the psychological impacts of social comparisons, and fostering resilience to appearance-related pressures. By advocating self-compassion and sustainable practices, fitness experts can assist clients in utilizing technology to enhance their well-being (Woessner et al., 2021).

Policy implications

Policymakers have the ability to improve user safety through the establishment of guidelines that advocate for ethical design, transparency in data, and support for mental health. Important policy areas encompass data privacy and protection, necessitating transparency in data usage, and introducing mental health safeguards such as warnings regarding potential psychological risks. Policies aimed at safeguarding vulnerable populations, enhancing accessibility, and fostering inclusivity are crucial for maintaining a harmonious digital health landscape (Limone & Toto, 2022).

Vision for the future of fitness technology

With the progression of fitness technology, there is the potential to promote a holistic approach to health that prioritizes physical fitness, mental strength, and self-kindness (Codina et al., 2024). Future advancements ought to incorporate mental health assistance elements, individualized adjustments to accommodate user preferences, and ethical advancements that emphasize user welfare and confidentiality (Ryan & Deci, 2020). Ensuring enhanced personalization, integration of mental health support, and ethical and inclusive development are crucial for the creation of effective and supportive tools.

Conclusion

The advancement of fitness technology is not solely dependent on tracking physical metrics but also on empowering users comprehensively, promoting resilience, and enhancing mental and emotional well-being. This vision necessitates continuous research, ethical advancement, and cooperation among developers, fitness experts, policymakers, and researchers. They can collectively steer the development of fitness technology as a catalyst for holistic health, enabling users to enhance their physical and mental well-being.

Chapter 11

FINAL REMARKS PART 2

Furthering the integration of fundamental discoveries from Part 1, Part 2 delves into the wider repercussions of these insights, exploring how the dual impact of fitness technology on motivation and social anxiety informs both user involvement and industry standards.

The primary research question driving this book is, *How does fitness technology influence users' physical self-concept and social physique anxiety in the context of regular fitness engagement?*

This book aimed to explore the advantages of utilizing fitness apps and wearable devices for self-monitoring and goal-setting, as well as the possible psychological risks, particularly in terms of social comparison and body image-related anxiety.

The hypothesis posited that fitness technology could improve physical self-concept by fostering autonomy, competence, and relatedness, yet it might also elevate social physique anxiety by encouraging social comparison. Social Comparison Theory and Self-Determination Theory offer a dual framework for exploring this hypothesis: the former proposes that users' body dissatisfaction and anxiety may increase through social comparison (Festinger, 1954), while the latter argues that intrinsic motivation and physical self-concept may improve as users achieve personalized fitness goals (Deci & Ryan, 1985; Ryan & Deci, 2020).

The results are consistent with the hypothesis, demonstrating that fitness technology has both empowering and harmful psychological impacts on users. Quantitative data indicated that elements promoting personal goal-setting and progress tracking improve physical self-concept (Marsh, 1996), often strengthening feelings of competence and satisfaction. Users expressed a sense of empowerment and motivation to maintain physical activity, supporting the constructive impact of feedback on improving physical self-perception (Codina et al., 2024).

On the other hand, the hypothesis regarding social physique anxiety was supported by qualitative and quantitative data, indicating that regular interaction with social elements like leaderboards or shared progress metrics is linked to higher levels of body dissatisfaction and self-awareness. This demonstrates the adverse effects of social comparison mechanisms present in fitness technology, consistent with the conclusions drawn by Crusius et al. (2022) and Zartaloudi et al. (2023).

The dual effect noted underscores the intricate function of fitness technology: as it promotes personal fitness accomplishments and self-assurance, it can also elevate social physique anxiety if individuals adopt societal norms and contrasts (Limone & Toto, 2022). Therefore, the book asserts that a well-rounded strategy in designing fitness technology, which prioritizes individual advancement over social comparison, is crucial in alleviating these psychological impacts, benefiting developers and users alike.

Chapter 12

FINAL REMARKS PART 3

Part 3 of the discussion transitions toward a forward-looking perspective, examining recommendations and future directions to promote a balanced and mindful approach in personal and societal settings.

Summary of Core Findings

Throughout the book, an examination of fitness technology has unveiled a complex dual influence on users' mental health. Despite the motivational advantages provided by fitness technology, especially with its goal-setting and tracking functions, there are potential risks associated with its social comparison components, such as social physique anxiety. Through the establishment of a structured setting enabling users to establish, monitor, and accomplish individualized objectives, fitness technology has successfully corresponded with Self-Determination Theory (Deci & Ryan, 1985), emphasizing the significance of fulfilling psychological needs for competence, autonomy, and relatedness (Ryan & Deci, 2020). By engaging in self-monitoring and utilizing data-driven feedback, users enhance their physical self-concept, as evidenced by the positive relationship between technology usage and self-concept (Marsh, 1996).

On the other hand, the incorporation of social comparison elements, like leaderboards, peer progress sharing, and social media integration, brings about a different psychological aspect. Social Comparison Theory (Festinger, 1954) provides understanding of this phenomenon by suggesting that individuals assess themselves by comparing with others, especially in areas lacking clear benchmarks (Crusius et al., 2022). Within the realm of fitness technology, this element may prompt users to critically assess themselves, particularly if they believe they are falling short of others' accomplishments (Limone & Toto, 2022). This contrast frequently intensifies social physique anxiety, an emotional reaction to perceived evaluation of one's physical appearance, with numerous subjects in this research noting increased self-awareness when observing the advancement of others (Zartaloudi et al., 2023).

Theoretical Integration

The optimal comprehension of the dual influence of fitness technology necessitates an amalgamation of three vital theoretical frameworks: Social Comparison Theory, Self-Determination Theory, and the Hierarchical Model of Physical Self-Concept. Social Comparison Theory elucidates the reasons behind users feeling motivated by peer accomplishments or experiencing self-doubt and anxiety. The competitive aspects of fitness technology platforms facilitate upward and downward social comparisons, with notable consequences for users' self-perceptions (Festinger, 1954). The Hierarchical Model of Physical Self-Concept (Marsh, 1996) elucidates this influence by emphasizing how technology nurtures distinct subdomains of self-concept, such as strength, endurance, and appearance, through the provision of real-time data on physical accomplishments (Oginni et al., 2024). Individuals have been found to experience higher levels of self-efficacy and satisfaction upon reaching fitness milestones. However, individuals may experience pressure when assessing their advancements against those of others, potentially causing a disturbance in their contentment with their physical image (Marsh, 1996).

Self-Determination Theory highlights the intrinsic motivation that technology can cultivate through user interaction with features promoting autonomy, competence, and relatedness (Deci & Ryan, 1985; Codina et al., 2024). Fitness technology empowers users to take charge of their fitness journeys and monitor customized progress, fostering a sense of responsibility for health outcomes and enhancing intrinsic motivation (Ryan & Deci, 2020). Nevertheless, with the increasing prevalence of social comparison elements, there is a possibility for a decrease in intrinsic motivation as individuals prioritize external validation, potentially leading to detrimental effects on mental well-being (Codina et al., 2024). Hence, these theories collectively elucidate the dual role of fitness technology as a motivational tool and a potential source of psychological pressure, contingent upon users' interaction with its different aspects.

Practical Implications

The results of this book emphasize important practical implications for various stakeholders, such as users, fitness professionals, developers, and policymakers. The research emphasizes the significance of overseeing engagement with social aspects for users, as focusing on comparative metrics may diminish intrinsic motivation and heighten social physique anxiety. Through prioritizing personalized objectives, individuals can leverage the motivational advantages of technology while avoiding the negative consequences linked to social comparisons (Zartaloudi et al., 2023). Establishing goals centered on performance, like achieving particular distances in running or specific weights in lifting, as opposed to appearance-based criteria, is in accordance with Self-Determination Theory and promotes individual development over seeking external approval (Ryan & Deci, 2020).

This study suggests that fitness professionals should prioritize assisting clients in establishing customized goals centered on functional fitness and resilience, rather than focusing on metrics based on appearance that could worsen social anxiety (Zartaloudi et al., 2023). Fitness professionals can encourage healthier self-concepts by redirecting clients' goals toward performance-oriented accomplishments, helping them find satisfaction in their progress rather than comparing themselves to others (Oginni et al., 2024). Furthermore, it is recommended that professionals inform clients about the possible impacts of social comparison in fitness technology, promoting a focus on internal accomplishments (Limone & Toto, 2022).

Developers play a crucial role in creating user-centered platforms that promote mental well-being, as evidenced by research on social physique anxiety related to comparative aspects (Zartaloudi et al., 2023). Implementing privacy settings, customizable social sharing options, and features that prioritize personal growth over public metrics could cultivate a psychologically supportive atmosphere. The design factors adhere to ethical principles that prioritize autonomy and user well-being (Ryan & Deci, 2020; Woessner et al., 2021). Furthermore, incorporating prompts that prompt users to reflect on personal accomplishments rather than seeking social approval can aid in sustaining motivation and mental well-being (Codina et al., 2024).

Policymakers must consider regulatory standards concerning data privacy, ethical design, and mental health safeguards in relation to fitness technology. Policymakers are advised to create regulations that enhance transparency in data utilization and safeguard mental health, ensuring that fitness technology acts as a beneficial influence in users' lives (Limone & Toto, 2022). By adhering to these guidelines, policymakers can contribute to establishing a fitness technology ecosystem that upholds user privacy and addresses the challenges linked to social comparison.

Future Research Directions

Further research is crucial to investigate the long-term psychological impacts of fitness technology. Longitudinal studies could offer valuable insights into the impact of sustained engagement on self-concept, motivation, and social anxiety. Knowing the trajectory of these psychological effects would provide a more nuanced comprehension of the influence of fitness technology on mental health (Codina et al., 2024). Furthermore, it is imperative to conduct cross-cultural studies to explore the global variations in social comparison and physical self-concept, as users' encounters are expected to be shaped by diverse cultural norms and expectations (Oginni et al., 2024).

Research should additionally investigate demographic-specific analyses, with a specific focus on age and gender, as societal pressures may intensify the impact of social physique anxiety on certain groups. Analyzing these differences could aid in the creation of inclusive technology that addresses the psychological requirements of various populations (Limone & Toto, 2022). In addition, forthcoming research could explore how personality characteristics like competitiveness or perfectionism influence reactions to fitness technology, providing insights into which individuals might be more susceptible to anxiety triggered by comparisons (Crusius et al., 2022).

Ethical Considerations

Developers and fitness professionals play a crucial role in upholding ethical responsibilities to promote a fitness technology ecosystem that prioritizes mental health. Ethical design in fitness technology ought to emphasize user autonomy, transparency, and mental well-being over engagement metrics, especially when incorporating social and comparative elements (Woessner et al., 2021). Developers are ethically responsible for designing platforms that empower users to establish personal goals and customize social features, promoting self-compassion and intrinsic motivation (Ryan & Deci, 2020).

Moreover, it is crucial to prioritize transparency regarding data usage, especially since fitness technology often depends on user-generated data for feedback. Policymakers and developers need to work together to set standards for data protection in order to instill confidence in users regarding their privacy when utilizing fitness technology (Limone & Toto, 2022). Adhering to these ethical standards is crucial in establishing a sustainable and supportive environment for users, where both physical and mental well-being are given equal importance (Zartaloudi et al., 2023).

Vision for the Future of Fitness Technology

In the future, fitness technology could aid in promoting a well-rounded, holistic approach to health that prioritizes physical, mental, and emotional well-being. By cultivating a setting that prioritizes internal drive and reduces comparisons, fitness technology has the potential to enhance users' resilience, self-belief, and self-kindness (Ryan & Deci, 2020). This advancement necessitates ongoing cooperation among users, experts, and developers, with a mutual dedication to establishing an all-encompassing and encouraging technological atmosphere (Woessner et al., 2021).

With the progression of digital health environments, the future of fitness technology hinges on its capacity to enhance holistic health and wellness. Through the creation of ethically designed platforms that prioritize mental health, intrinsic motivation, and user-centered features, the industry can establish a positive environment that enables users to pursue sustainable health goals effectively. The goal is to establish a fitness technology culture that celebrates personal growth and self-acceptance, ensuring that fitness journeys are rooted in user-centered values rather than external validation (Codina et al., 2024).

In conclusion, this final section promotes a future in which fitness technology enhances psychological resilience, self-compassion, and overall health, prioritizing users' well-being over engagement metrics. By means of deliberate design, mindful regulation, and user education, the fitness technology sector has the capability to empower individuals in their pursuit of holistic physical and mental well-being.

REFERENCES

Bandura, A. (1977). Self-efficacy: Toward a unifying theory of behavioral change. *Psychological Review, 84*(2), 191–215. https://doi.org/10.1037/0033-295X.84.2.191

Braun, V., & Clarke, V. (2006). Using thematic analysis in psychology. *Qualitative Research in Psychology, 3*(2), 77–101. https://doi.org/10.1191/1478088706qp063oa

British Educational Research Association. (2018, June 20). *Ethical guidelines for educational research* (4th ed.). https://www.bera.ac.uk/publication/ethical-guidelines-for -educational-research-2018

Codina, N., Valenzuela, R., & Pestana, J. V. (2024). All physical activities are not created equal: Differential effects of goal contents, psychological need satisfaction, and flow in physical activity on satisfaction with life. *Current Psychology, 43*. https://doi.org/10 .1007/s12144-024-05678-2

Crusius, J., Corcoran, K., & Mussweiler, T. (2022). Social comparison. In D. Chadee (Ed.), *Theories in social psychology* (2nd ed., pp. 165–187). Wiley. https://doi.org/10.1002 /9781394266616.ch7

Deci, E. L., & Ryan, R. M. (1985). *Intrinsic motivation and self-determination in human behavior.* Plenum.

Festinger, L. (1954). A theory of social comparison processes. *Human Relations, 7*(2), 117– 140. https://doi.org/10.1177/001872675400700202

Gernigon, C., Hartigh, R. J. R. D., Vallacher, R. R., & Geert, P. L. C. van. (2023). How the complexity of psychological processes reframes the issue of reproducibility in psychological science. *Perspectives on Psychological Science, 19*(6). https://doi.org/10 .1177/17456916231187324

Limone, P., & Toto, G. A. (2022). Psychological and emotional effects of digital technology on digitods (14–18 Years): A systematic review. *Frontiers in Psychology, 13*. https://doi .org/10.3389/fpsyg.2022.938965

Marsh, H. W. (1996). Physical self description questionnaire: Stability and discriminant validity. *Research Quarterly for Exercise and Sport, 67*(3), 249–264. https://doi.org/10.1080 /02701367.1996.10607952

Oginni, J., Otinwa, G., & Gao, Z. (2024). Physical impact of traditional and virtual physical exercise programs on health outcomes among corporate employees. *Journal of Clinical Medicine, 13*(3), 694–694. https://doi.org/10.3390/jcm13030694

Ratan, S., Anand, T., & Ratan, J. (2019). Formulation of research question – Stepwise approach. *Journal of Indian Association of Pediatric Surgeons, 24*(1), 15–20. NCBI. https:// pmc.ncbi.nlm.nih.gov/articles/PMC6322175/

Ryan, R. M., & Deci, E. L. (2020). Intrinsic and extrinsic motivation from a self-determination theory perspective: Definitions, theory, practices, and future directions. *Contemporary Educational Psychology, 61*(1), 1–11. https://doi.org/10.1016/j.cedpsych.2020.101860

The British Psychological Society. (2018). Code of ethics and conduct. In *BPS.org.uk*. https://www.bps.org.uk/news-and-policy/bps-code-ethics-and-conduct

Woessner, M. N., Tacey, A., Levinger-Limor, A., Parker, A. G., Levinger, P., & Levinger, I. (2021). The evolution of technology and physical inactivity: The good, the bad, and the way forward. *Frontiers in Public Health, 9*. https://doi.org/10.3389/fpubh.2021.655491

Woll, A., Cleven, L., Jekauc, D., Krell-Roesch, J., & Bös, K. (2023). A tool to assess fitness among adults in public health studies – Predictive validity of the FFB-Mot questionnaire. *BMC Public Health, 23*(1). https://doi.org/10.1186/s12889-023-16174-w

Zartaloudi, A., Christopoulos, D., Kelesi, M., Govina, O., Mantzorou, M., Adamakidou, T., Karvouni, L., Koutelekos, I., Evangelou, E., Fasoi, G., & Vlachou, E. (2023). Body image, social physique anxiety levels and self-esteem among adults participating in physical activity programs. *Diseases, 11*(2), 66. https://doi.org/10.3390/diseases11020066

www.ingramcontent.com/pod-product-compliance
Lightning Source LLC
Chambersburg PA
CBHW031447280326
41927CB00037B/390